TWAYNE'S WORLD AUTHORS SERIES
A Survey of the World's Literature

SPAIN

Janet W. Diaz, Texas Tech University
and Gerald E. Wade

EDITORS

Nicolás Fernández de Moratín

TWAS 558

Flumisbo Thermodonciaco.

P. A.

Moratín el Padre

Nicolás Fernández de Moratín

NICOLÁS FERNÁNDEZ de MORATÍN

By DAVID THATCHER GIES

University of Virginia

TWAYNE PUBLISHERS
A DIVISION OF G. K. HALL & CO., BOSTON

Copyright © 1979 by G. K. Hall & Co.

Published in 1979 by Twayne Publishers,
A Division of G. K. Hall & Co.
All Rights Reserved

Printed on permanent/durable acid-free paper and bound
in the United States of America

First Printing

Library of Congress Cataloging in Publication Data

Gies, David Thatcher
Nicolás Fernández de Moratín.

(Twayne's world authors series ; TWAS 558 : Spain)
Bibliography: p. 173–79
Includes index.
1. Moratín, Nicolás Fernández de, 1737–1780 — Criticism and
interpretation.
PQ6549.M2Z67   868'.4'09   79-14980
ISBN 0-8057-6400-3

For Heather Whitney, whom I hope to meet someday

Contents

About the Author

David Thatcher Gies is Associate Professor of Spanish at the University of Virginia. He received his B.A. degree from the Pennsylvania State University and his M.A. and Ph.D. degrees from the University of Pittsburgh. Professor Gies has participated in numerous regional, national, and international conferences. He is a corresponding editor of the Purdue University Monographs in Romance Languages. His works include *Agustín Durán: A Biography and Literary Appreciation* (London, 1975), scholarly articles in *Cithara, Modern Language Studies,* and *Neohelicon,* and book reviews in *Cithara, Hispanic Review, Hispania,* and *Bulletin of Hispanic Studies.* He is currently working on a book on Spanish Romanticism.

Preface

We have generally known Nicolás Fernández de Moratín only through the veil that his son Leandro draped around him. The *Life* of his father, which he wrote in 1821 to introduce his edition of his father's *Posthumous Works,* is beautiful but biased, and many of the poems we read as Nicolás's are in fact reworkings published by his son. Indeed, it has been said and repeated that Nicolás's grandest creation was his son, the incomparable Leandro. Perhaps there is some truth in the statement; still, the pejorative implication of it is hardly fair, and severely limits our ability to perceive Moratín, the father, as a man and as an author. He was, after all, one of the most influential and highly regarded literary figures of his time, a time which has become known in retrospect as that of Neoclassicism.

In 1955 Edith Helman summed up the modern attitude toward the elder Moratín: "[He] is rapidly dispached by most literary historians, after a few cursory remarks about his jejune dramas and dramatic theory, into a kind of neo-classical limbo."[1] Most of the old clichés regarding the Spanish eighteenth century have been abandoned in recent years; contemporary criticism has succeeded in overturning outdated and unjust opinions of Spanish eighteenth-century literature. We are beginning to realize that it is not so cold, sterile (whatever does this mean?), Frenchified, or imitative as we were once led — nay, told — to believe. Yet some old saws are abandoned with difficulty, as a review of the criticism will demonstrate.

The traditional image of the eighteenth-century intellectual conjures up a figure in powdered wig, endlessly posturing in a literary salon or furiously reforming everything in sight. Reality is something quite different, but in the case of Moratín, how does one objectively approach a man who has been called the coldest and most vapid writer of his generation while also being considered the most influential writer of his day? What are we to do with critical views that pronounce his poetry boring yet claim that he wrote the best poems produced in eighteenth-century Spain? Where does the truth lie for an individual who considered himself a profound patriot and still was vilified as a literary turncoat? How do we analyze the productions of a writer whose theories helped to redirect the very flow of Spanish literature but who could not even get his own plays, with one exception, produced? The contradictions abound.

Nicolás Fernández de Moratín is a man of impressive successes and flamboyant failures, who forced people to look to higher standards of theatrical and poetical activity. Elsewhere I have argued the injustice of judging historical literary matters by modern standards. Here I shall likewise attempt to present Moratín within the framework of his own world which it is hoped will enable us to view more clearly what he did, what influence he had in his time, and what lasting impact, if any, he had on succeeding literary generations. Modernity gives us a valuable perspective and that perspective will be utilized in order to evaluate Moratín and his writings, but his successes and failures will be judged on their own. It will be necessary to suppress preconceived notions of Neoclassicism in order to understand and to analyze what Moratín considered literature to be and in order to study how he applied theory to his own productions. My purpose is to synthesize into a coherent whole the many and disparate writings by and on Moratín, and to add new information to the picture. From that, it is hoped that we will understand him, and his age, a little better.

This book is the first dedicated exclusively to Nicolás Fernández de Moratín. As such, and in keeping with the goals of the Twayne World Author Series, it must necessarily be an introduction. It is built upon the works of many other scholars whose contributions are sincerely acknowledged. My own research has taken me to more than twenty-six archives and libraries in the United States, Spain, and England, and I wish to thank the kind people in those countries whose dedication facilitated access to materials. I am especially grateful to those at the Biblioteca Nacional, Archivo de Palacio, Real Academia Española, Ateneo de Madrid, Real Sociedad Económica, Boston Public Library, New York Public Library, and the British Library for their help. Doña María Brey de Rodríguez-Moñino receives a special thank-you.

I am grateful also to the National Endowment for the Humanities for providing me with a research grant to continue the intermediate stages of my research, and to Professor Russell P. Sebold, whose own studies are so enlightening and who so patiently

Preface

read my manuscript and offered many informative suggestions. Last, I publicly acknowledge the dedication of my typist, whose hard work enabled the manuscript to make it through several drafts.

DAVID THATCHER GIES

University of Virginia

Chronology

Neoclassical theater, Moratín's tragedy *Hormesinda,* staged in Madrid. March 31: Nicolás and his wife make a pauper's will. December: Competition for the new Chair in Poetics at the Imperial College; Nicolás defeated by Ignacio López de Ayala.

1771   Writes scandalous *El arte de las putas.* Publishes four poems in praise of Garcilaso.

1771?   Tertulia at the Fonda de San Sebastián, attended by many leading literary figures.

1772?   Writes famous "Fiesta de toros en Madrid." Enters Madrid lawyers' bar.

1773   October: Ayala ill; Nicolás will replace him as Professor of Poetry at the Imperial College, and keep the position until his own death.

1775   Writes now-lost comedy, *La defensa de Melilla.*

1776   July: Writes a defense of the bullfight.

1777   Tragedy *Guzmán el Bueno* published. *El arte de las putas* manuscript placed on the *Index.*

1777–   Active membership in the new Real Sociedad Económica de
1780   Madrid. Writes and recites annual poems in praise of the Society's activities.

1778   March: Manuscript of "Las naves de Cortés, destruidas" handed in for the competition of the Real Academia Española; loses to José María Vaca de Guzmán.

1780   May 11: Dies in Madrid.

1785   "Las naves de Cortés, destruidas" published by Leandro.

1802   *Guzmán el Bueno* translated into English.

1821   Leandro collects, edits, revises, and publishes his father's works in *Obras póstumas,* Barcelona, together with an informative *Vida* of Don Nicolás.

1825   *Obras póstumas* published in London.

1846   The complete works of Nicolás published in Volume 2 of the *Biblioteca de Autores Españoles.*

CHAPTER 1

A Short Life

I   *From Madrid to Madrid*

IN 1719 Diego Fernández de Moratín deeded to prove that he was a *cristiano viejo* (old Christian) of noble lineage. From Madrid he contacted his cousin Pedro Fernández in Salas (province of Oviedo) to take care of the paperwork by arranging the witnesses and getting the necessary statements drawn up. Pedro gathered together six of the town's old men, who dutifully swore to the facts as they remembered them. All of these men — Antonio Fernández, seventy-four years old "more or less"[1]; Gregorio Alvarez de Lorada, seventy-eight; Juan Fernández del Vaneyro, seventy-nine; Toribio García, eighty; Nicolás García de Lorada, eighty-nine; and Pedro Alvarez de la Rebollada, ninety-three — teetered into the village to recount before a scribe that Diego was the legitimate son of Domingo, who had left the village in 1650 to seek his fortunes in Madrid, and that he in turn was the legitimate son of Tomás, who was the legitimate son of still another Domingo, and so on. Collectively they recalled information from the first third of the seventeenth century. The certification was performed with the utmost solemnity: after the testimonies were accepted (April 27 and 28, 1719), the scribe entered the local archives in the presence of the judge, the town clerk, a state attorney, and two aldermen to locate and to document the given facts, which he did, beginning with the books dated 1611–44. In 1789, a century and a half after the appearance of the first Domingo, his great-great-great grandson, Leandro Fernández de Moratín, ordered the testimonies to be recopied, and he appended to them his own baptismal record, as well as those of his grandfather Diego and of his father, Nicolás.

Thus we know that Nicolás Fernández de Moratín was born in Madrid on July 20, 1737. His family name was actually Fernández. The family was of old Asturian stock from a small town outside

15

Oviedo, a place called Moratín,[2] and subsequent generations of the "Fernández from Moratín" family integrated the place name into the family name itself. Hence, when his grandfather came to Madrid in 1650 he was known as Domingo Fernández or Domingo Fernández de Moratín. Even Nicolás would later, as late as 1776, write a treatise on agriculture under the semipseudonym of Rafael (his second name) Fernández. But it is the place name which has stuck, and consequently he and his son are known simply as Moratín the Elder and Moratín the Younger. 1737 was an auspicious year for Spanish Neoclassicism. Nicolás arrived just as Ignacio de Luzán was publishing his famous manifesto, *La poética,* and as the intriguing debate on the subject got underway in the *Diario de los Literatos de España* (Journal of Spanish Literati). The coincidence was not in vain since Nicolás would grow up to be one of the most ardent defenders of Neoclassicism and one of the movement's leading creative artists.

Nicolás's father, Diego, was baptized in Lope de Vega's church (San Ginés) in 1688. He outlived his first wife and married again on March 29, 1735. Inés González Cordón, twenty-nine, was the daughter of a family of landed gentry from Pastrana; Diego was forty-seven. They settled down to live in Madrid, and two years later their first son, Nicolás, was born. Diego made a living as one of the jewelkeepers to the reigning Bourbon family,[3] where he gained the respect and confidence of the queen, Isabel de Farnesio. This shrewd, brilliant, and cultured lady asked the Moratín family to continue their service to her in her retirement at La Granja, following the death of her husband, Felipe V, in 1746. They went, and the circumstances were good ones for young Nicolás. He befriended Prince Luis and was constantly exposed to the interests of Isabel. Very cosmopolitan interests they were, too: Isabel, of Italian background, member of the French royal family, and speaker of six or seven languages, created an atmosphere of cultured gentility at the palace. At La Granja Nicolás learned to read Spanish Classical authors — Lope, Calderón, Góngora, Quevedo — and became particularly enthusiastic about the *comedia* and *autos sacramentales* (allegorical religious dramas) of the Golden Age, an enthusiasm he later regretted and tried to blame on the corrupt tastes of one of his aunts.[4] Here his cosmopolitan tastes began to develop. As an adult he was known as an admirer (some say fanatic) of international culture and as an enthusiast (some say enemy) of Spanish literature.

The queen recognized in him a gracious intelligence and encouraged Diego, who was known to scribble some verses himself,[5] to have Nicolás study literature; she even offered to pay for his education. So he was sent off to pursue his studies at the Jesuit school in Calatayud, mixing vacations and summers with his "families" at La Granja, taking joy at seeing his younger brothers and sister — Miguel, Manuel, and Ana (born in 1748 when her father was sixty years old) — who remained at home.[6] Calatayud had a fine reputation in those days; it was "a school for nobles in which were educated the most select members of Aragonese society,"[7] among them José Pignatelli, with whom Moratín would later make acquaintence, the famous Jesuit José Antonio Masdeu, and others. From there he went on to the University of Valladolid, where he presented the necessary proofs for admission (grammar, rhetoric, philosophy, Latin — in short, a standard education) and matriculated at the age of sixteen into the law school,[8] under the name of Nicolás Rafael Fernández. Biographical "information," presumably taken from Leandro's *Vida* of his father — although Leandro merely says that his father "studied" law — repeats that Moratín graduated with his law degree (he has even been granted a doctoral degree by some). Yet there is reason to raise doubts about the official nature of those statements, for his sole appearances in the archives of the university are those relating to his presentation of credentials. He does not appear in any of the books, records, or documents which I saw, other than the two mentioned, nor does he appear in the university's records of degrees awarded. Philip Deacon claims to have information indicating that Moratín purchased the needed degree at Osma.[9]

Back at La Granja, Moratín entertained the queen and her son Luis with poems he had written, and regaled them with animated tales of student life. He was given a position as an assistant jewel-keeper. Once he had a career, or at least a stable job that would provide security, he was able to marry. The girl of his choice was from Aldeaseca (a dusty little town in the province of Avila), and a charming and attractive girl she was. At twenty, just one year younger than Nicolás, Isidora Cabo Conde met with the immediate approval of his parents and of the queen. When Fernando VI died on August 10, 1759, without an heir, Isabel was called back to Madrid to await the arrival of the new king, her son and Fernando's half-brother, Carlos III. Naturally the Moratíns accompanied her to the capital, where they settled down on San Juan

Street, in the Plaza de San Juan neighborhood, in a house which still stands today. Carlos triumphantly entered the city on December 9, 1759; soon everything was to change, from the direction of Spanish politics to the focus of Nicolás's literary ideas and activities.

II *Into the Fray*

Moratín claims that he knew nothing of Madrid when he returned in 1759. In the guise of Lucindo in his poem "Egloga a Velasco y González" (Eclogue to Velasco and González) he states: "I, although born in Madrid, / Was deprived of seeing it / By a drawn-out absence."[10] Yet he had spent the first nine years of his life there, since the family did not retire to La Granja until 1746. Nevertheless, it is impossible to dispute his claim since almost nothing is known about those early years. Isidora was then carrying their first child. A new stage of Nicolas's life was beginning. Madrid was to him a revelation: "Ignorant, I believed / That it would be like our village"[11] and not a huge, beautiful, and exciting city, brimming with activity. Madrid was alive:

> Mas lo que arrebató la atención mía,
> Fue el saber que aquel día
> Las artes nobles bellas
> De la naturaleza imitadoras,
> Hermanas de la docta poesía,
> Con honrosa porfía
> Al mismo original aventajaban.
> . . .
> La gran corte hermosea
> Con tantos edificios,
> Que yo para contarlos desaliento.[12]

> (But what captured my attention
> Was knowning that that day
> Noble fine arts,
> Imitators of nature,
> Sisters of learned poetry,
> With honorable obstinacy
> Surpassed the original itself.
> . . .
> The court shimmers in beauty
> With so many edifices
> That I lose my breath counting them.)

He toured the capital's libraries, went to the theater, joined in festivities, and learned where the centers of influence and power lay. He went to the bullfights, whose excitement and danger inspired in him some of his most eloquent writings. He was immediately struck by the charm and intelligence of the people he met, no doubt aided by his favored position in the queen mother's household. Within a few months of his arrival, as Leandro tells it,[13] he met such literary and artistic luminaries as musician Luis Misón, sculptor Felipe de Castro, critic and poet Luis Velázquez, ecclesiastical historian Enrique Flórez, dramatist Agustín Montiano, bibliophile Juan de Iriarte, and the theatrical sisters María and Francisca Ladvenant. The men were the core of Neoclassical Madrid (not yet thought of as such, of course), and some were members of the rather overconfidently named Academy of Good Taste: Castro had decorated the impressive Royal Palace ("I can't even describe to you that wonder / Of beauty, artistic admiration, / Sumptuous castle"[14]); Velázquez, the Marquis of Valdeflores, five years earlier had published his *Orígenes de la poesía castellana* (Origins of Spanish Poetry); Father Flórez was compiling his interminable *España sagrada* (Sacred Spain). But it was the last individuals — Montiano, Iriarte, Francisca Ladvenant — who impressed him the most and who were to be, in very different ways, central to the shaping of his literary destiny. What singled Moratín out, aside from his vehemence, good contacts, and obvious brilliance, was his youth — except for his singing friend Francisca and her actress sister, the others were old, and all would be dead within fifteen years.

Leandro was born March 10, 1760. Moratín the Younger was to become so famous that Mesonero Romanos would call him Nicolás's "most enduring production,"[15] and until now he has been the sole reason for most readers' interest in his father. The neighborhood in which he was born was an interesting one. Mesonero dubbed it the "neighborhood of the muses" — it is just around the corner from the Príncipe and Cruz theaters, and many notable Spaniards had been born or lived there, including Cervantes, Lope, and Calderón, and in the Moratíns' time, María Ladvenant and other stage people such as La Tirana, Isidoro Máiquez, and Rita Luna. Leandro mentions it in his own *La comedia nueva o el Café* (The New Comedy or the Café), although his most distinct childhood memories were from the house on Santa Isabel Street, across Atocha, where they moved before he was a year old.

When not engaged in family matters or with his job, Nicolás began to write, heavily influenced by the growing Neoclassical trends dominant in the circles with which he associated himself. Notwithstanding Leandro's crack that Luzán's *Poetics* was not read in 1760, Nicolás perceived great merit in the move toward more closely regulated theater and poetry. The introductory discourse he wrote for his first play, *La petimetra* (The Petimetra)[16] of 1762, clearly stated his guiding principles, which soundly squared with those that Montiano had voiced previously: to "purge" playwriting of impropriety, to use Classical authors as models, and to guard such standards as decorum, verisimilitude, the three unities, and the imitation of nature. These ideas were discussed in the *tertulias* and literary salons of the capital, partially because of the attempted originality of the piece to which they were attached: *La petimetra* was the first Spanish comedy ever written "according to the rules." But the play itself was not a success, so Moratín turned toward a more tried, if equally unsuccessful, formla — tragedy.

Lucrecia (Lucretia) appeared the following year, 1763, with another prologue, and Moratín, apparently sensitive to criticisms he had received about *La petimetra,* reinforced even more stridently his support of rules, rules, rules. He did, however, try to protect his flanks by admitting to certain errors or weaknesses in his dramas while at the same time repeating his conviction of the rightness of his position: "It appeared to me that our comedies were extremely foolish due to the abandonment of the rules of theater; and so I was not content merely to point them out, but rather, as I could, I put them to use. Now I am doing the same thing with tragedies. Whoever may think mine is bad, I beg him to do another...."[17] He prides himself on sticking to the rules here, too, yet the play was received with the same indifference as *La petimetra.*

At about this same time Nicolás was drawn into a debate concerning the value of Spanish Golden Age theater. His published comments were vitriolic enough to earn him the enmity of certain contemporaries as well as that of generations of critics. Even today he is labeled "antinational"[18] and "an enemy of Spanish theater,"[19] although clearly he was neither. The first of his *Desengaños al teatro español* (Reproaches to the Spanish Theater) appeared in response to a poem written to attack José Clavijo y Fajardo's *El Pensador* (The Thinker), a series of "thoughts" in which are contained some rather harsh criticisms of Spanish

Golden Age plays. Moratín, writing from La Granja and disclaiming any vested interest ("I do not know the author of the *Thinker,* nor of the poem"), sided with Clavijo, and within a year produced two more *Reproaches,* the last two of which were directed against the "defects" of Calderón's one-act religious plays, the *autos sacramentales.* Even though Leandro overstated the case by suggesting that his father's *Reproaches* caused the eventual abolition of these dramas, there can be no doubt that they were pivotal in creating an official climate favorable to the Neoclassicists' ideas.

January 1764 saw the appearance of Moratín's first published verse collection, a cleverly conceived poetry periodical called *El Poeta Matritense* (The Madrilenian Poet). This was to be a weekly publication, although in reality it appeared sporadically since its ten numbers took two years to come out. The first issue was very short, containing just two poems and a prologue, but it was revealing. His point of departure is purely Classical here, and in the prologue, even before mentioning Spanish poetry, he has called upon the authority of Pindar, Homer, Marcial, Ovid, and Horace. "I do not deny," he writes, "that we have excellent Spanish poets who can compare with the best not only from Italy and France, but from ancient Rome and Greece: but it is also true that their works have been lost, and some can be found only at great difficulty and expense."[20] And, he adds, the great poets Spain has had have been smothered by the inundation of versifiers and rhymesters, those ubiquitous individuals who think one need only grab a group of consonants to produce verses by the dozen. "I once knew an idiot, a man who could scarcely read, who spewed forth innumerable rhymes so rapidly that he could follow any simple conversation in verse; but he did it without enthusiasm, invention, art, study, or imitation, or any of the other requisites of a poet: his entire skill consisted in rhyming common statements which should have been kept in simple prose. Anyone who believes that poetry is reduced to this will not appreciate my work."[21] Yet in the very first poem, a type of *ars poetica,* he writes more of enjoyment than of instruction, hoping to "please," "content," "give pleasure to," and "humor" his readers, a goal which he reaches in many of them. In this first poem lie the cleverness, the possible contradictions, and the ultimate failure of Moratín. The seeds of his whole poetic conception can be found here: enjoyment, instruction (he hopes to avoid pedantry; in many poems he does, but others are riddled and eventually ruined by his torrent of learned references; he also

changes his mind later on with a kind of to-hell-with-fools attitude), Classical models, and, perhaps most important, national
themes. He intends to sing of Spanish kings and heroes ("My
numerous verses will praise / The country and her most famous
sons"), as well as local customs, loves, wars, and certain "truths"
— in short, an amalgam of themes and concerns. Only fifty-three
poems were published in the *Poet;* the rest of his poetic production,
with a few exceptions, did not reach print until forty-one years
after his death when Leandro published his father's *Obras
póstumas* (Posthumous Works) in Barcelona in 1821. But Nicolás's
reputation as a poet grew steadily during the decade of the 1760s,
and by the 1770s he was widely acclaimed as one of the country's
leading poets.

   Their first four years in Madrid had not been particularly kind to
the Moratín family. Smallpox almost killed Leandro in 1764, and
his serious illness was a tragic blow; it also brought up painful
memories of the three other children Isidora had borne Nicolás —
Miguel, María, Facundo — who died so young that Leandro was
moved to say that he hardly knew them. Small wonder, then, that
Nicolás developed a strict regime of discipline and study for his
only surviving son, from whom he expected great things. The boy
was exceptionally bright, anyway, learning to read at a very early
age, but Nicolás apparently feared that the constant devotion
shown him by his doting mother and grandparents would somehow
hinder his intellectual development. First a tutor came to the house,
then later he was put under the guarded tutelage of a schoolmaster,
Santiago López, who lived down the street and whom Leandro
remembered with less than total affection. "Guarded" applies because Nicolás did not entirely trust the educational "system" of his
day (i.e., "scholastic philosophy" taught in the Jesuit institutions,
anathema to the new enlightened thinkers), and therefore watched
closely and joined in the instruction of his son. Nicolás directed his
reading from his own rich library and surrounded him with the ac-
coutrements of his own literary world, that which would become
known as Neoclassicism. Silvela records, quoting Leandro,
Nicolás's reaction to the suggestion that the boy be sent away to
study: "I am pleased with the lad; I do not want to send him anywhere where he might be ruined."[22] It is not without foundation
that Professor Dowling writes that the "literary creation of
Leandro, indeed, represents a constitution and a refinement of efforts initiated by his father."[23]

Nicolás was strict and watchful, but to characterize him as a near monster, as Patricio de la Escosura does in the nineteenth century — complete with references to Leandro's alleged "antipathy to the abuses of paternal authority" and "submission to the total authority of his enlightened father" — is unjust. Nicolás had his son learn a skill, that of jewelmaking, to complement his studies and to provide a back-up occupation if he ever needed one; Nicolás well knew the tenuousness of a literary existence. Escosura hysterically reports it this way: "So young Leandro, whom God had created for literature, was condemned to learn and to practice a mechanical job.... Is it any wonder that family absolutism would be anathema to a man educated in such circumstances?"[24] The irony of the statement is that, although Leandro did not like the job, it was a good thing that he could do something to earn money, since when his father died in 1780 the family was penniless and Leandro was left with the burden of supporting himself and his mother. He turned precisely to this trade. The image of being a stern father has remained with Nicolás, yet there is little hint of it in Leandro's writings; he himself fondly remembers and gives testimony to the enormous and beneficial influence of his father: "[At home] I saw my father's friends, heard their literary conversations, and there acquired an excessive love for study. I read *Don Quijote, Lazarillo,* the *Guerras de Granada* [Wars of Granada], a delicious book for me, the *Historia* of Mariana, and all the Spanish poets, which my father's library contained in abundance."[25]

A long, instructive poem entitled *La Diana o el arte de la caza* (Diana or the Art of the Hunt) appeared in 1765 while his verse periodical was still appearing. Didactic treatises in verse were fashionable in his day, if not necessarily popular, and this one certainly addressed itself to the favorite pastime of the king. It was also another salvo in his continuing preoccupation with "worthy" poetry, exemplifying his own most deeply felt tenet: that only he who produces art, or attempts to provide respectable examples of it, has the right to criticize it. Aware of his own models, he admits that it is not a new thing to deal with the various "sciences" in verse form.[26] One wonders to whom he directed this prologue (indeed one wonders to whom he directed any of them), interspersed as it is not simply with references to well-known figures such as Virgil and Lucretius, but to the likes of Hesiod and Cardinal de Polignac, and liberally sprinkled with Latin quotations. But there, of course, is the answer. He obviously is addressing himself to the educated strata of Spanish literary society, those who criticize and those who write, in order to produce a reform which would filter down to the people. He does so in a patronizing manner, saying for example that certain quotations will be omitted since the know-nothings will not understand them anyway, and the knowledgeable should not need them. Another key to his poetic technique is revealed when he writes: "If a certain work employs a pure language, poetic sentences, solid thoughts and natural elegance, then people should look upon it reverently even though they may not understand certain allusions to fable or history or other similar erudite things; after all, the poet cannot be held responsible for the lack of education on his readers' part."[27] So it is form and content that are essential: proper (Neoclassical) form, and proper (instructive) content.

Nicolás by this time had acquired a reputation as a knowledgeable, aggressive, and partisan defender of Classical ideals. But how successful were the campaigns? His archenemy Ramón de la Cruz enjoyed such popularity that he felt free to do battle with Moratín and his group; in fact, he brutally satirized him in one of his *sainetes,* making him out to be quite the stuffy and foolish pedant.[28] No doubt the characterization had some exaggerated truth to it, if we keep in mind Ramón de la Cruz's own aggressive talent for satire: the "genius" is presented as poor, sickly, arrogant, and convinced that he alone bears the standard for excellence in Art: "The folly of this man / Betters that of many / Others, for he alone / Wants to carry the day / In all areas, his own / As well as those of others, / Making everyone in the / World restrict himself / To his rules and his teachings." This does, indeed, confirm some of what we know to be true. But personality alone does not rule; power does, and Moratín had well-connected friends. As noted, the campaign against the *autos* resulted in their being banned in 1765, and with the arrival of the liberal Count Aranda in 1767, the leaders of Neoclassicism saw their ideas transformed into realities.

The death of Isabel de Farnesio ("ever strong Semiramis"[29]) in 1766 was a personal blow to Moratín. He had lived in her household, grown up in her shadow, and prospered under her tutelage. Her sons were his friends. His grief was deep. When the ninth issue of the *Poet* appeared, it brought with it his elegy "A la muerte de la reina madre Isabel Farnesio" (On the Death of the Queen Mother, Isabel Farnesio). The initial tercets express Moratín's confusion, sadness, and sense of frustration in a way that can almost be described as Romantic. Two interrogatives, a stylistic device that he often used, lead into a second stanza in which nature itself reacts to the queen mother's death ("I watch the land full of tears, / With sighs and anxiety the wind blushes, / A hoarse moan sounds throughout the earth"[30]). The sadness and melancholy are underlined with lugubrious references to a "mournful owl" and a "scarab," all bathed, of course, in "tears," "mourning," and "horror." He is not a whimpering versifier, sniffling his anguish; on the contrary, the beginning of the poem is aggressive. He is overtly hostile to the "tyranny" of death. Yet the poem is soon deflated to convention, enumerating Isabel's successes while enhancing them with mythological allusions. Only once does he regain our full attention and manage to make us identify with his sorrow: as he turns toward Isabel, he speaks with her "one last time": "Where have you gone? Have we served you so poorly? / Thus you leave your children and servants / In affliction and eternal oblivion?" We accept this abandonment, and we are moved by his loss. He self-consciously incorporates a verse of Garcilaso, inserting word for word the opening line of the Tenth Sonnet, and calls himself Isabel's "swan," ironically aware of a reversal in that he now sings her swan song. He does not, however, maintain the fury or the tenderness throughout the poem's 325 verses.

Moratín had been schooled by the Jesuits but his real education was a result of his life in the court of Isabel and in the literary atmosphere of Madrid. He was not particularly attracted to the ritualistic religious pageantry of the established Church, although naturally he was a parish member. His sympathies lay with those of more reform-minded laymen (he could not help but be influenced by Rousseau), whose emphasis was evident in the new scientific rationalism that was the hallmark of enlightened thought. Yet he was far from antagonistic to the Church. He refused to participate in the pamphleteering against the Jesuits which became so popular in 1767, even when asked to do so directly by Aranda (who, while not happy with Moratín's decision, respected it). Their friendship even grew, and a few years later Moratín sent to the count a Pindaric ode praising this new "Aquilles," "Eneas," "Scipion," and "Licurgus," noting that "he who loves poetry is worthy of poetry."[31]

III   *Success?*

Moratín continued to enlarge his circle of friends. The family moved across town to Puebla Street (today called Fomento) in the Encarnación area, right up the street from the Royal Library, into a building that also housed the Italian Ignacio Bernascone. Cultured and genteel, Bernascone became a fast friend of Moratín's and soon introduced him to a compatriot, Juan Bautista Conti. From there the circle widened. Conti, in Madrid since 1765, was an old friend, since his school days in Bologna, of the botanist Casimiro Gómez Ortega. Another Italian, Pietro Napoli Signorelli, had likewise arrived in Spain's capital in 1765. José Cadalso was back in Madrid from his exile, in love with the gracious María Ignacia Ibáñez. Moratín was impressed with their knowledge and support of Neoclassical ideas, and they were all struck with his glib brilliance. When joined by Tomás de Iriarte, Ignacio López de Ayala, and Francisco Cerdá y Rico, they became the most potent force in the literary activities of the city. Moratín's poetry had gained him prominence, and people read his publications. A collection of his prose and verse works "on matters of pleasure and usefulness" was announced in the *Gaceta de Madrid* in August of 1769.

Perhaps the crowning "successes" of the Neoclassical group were two occurrences, both in 1770. One was the staging of Nicolás's original verse tragedy, *Hormesinda,* and the other was Ayala's capture, at Nicolás's expense, of the Poetry Chair at the newly restructured Imperial College of San Isidro. No matter that Nicolás lost the bid for the position. Ayala was part of the "in" group, and the ideas mattered most. Besides, Nicolás eventually got the chair by default when Ayala became too ill to tend to his teaching duties.

Moratín refused to let setbacks defeat him, although he suffered enough of them to justify any bitterness he may have felt toward his enemies. That *La petimetra* and *Lucrecia* had never been brought to life on the stage did not deter him from another attempt to bring the rules of the theater *into* the theater. The time was riper, too. Aranda was a strong patron of theatrical reform, and official recognition resulted in the creation of special royal theaters designed to encourage "correct" theater. Many of Moratín's friends were involved in the new projects as translators or as rewriters. The king seemed somewhat interested (well, tolerant), and the power elite and court hangers-on generally go where the official wind leads them. So *Hormesinda* was produced, if not without difficulties. Moratín asked María Ignacia Ibáñez to play the lead role, which she accepted only after some remonstrations of inability, lack of experience, etc. But the members of the acting company put up the stiffest opposition (as they had done with his earlier plays), based on their own dislike for what they called the "French style." Leandro recounts the amusing, and revealing, anecdote of José Espejo trying to talk Moratín into adding a *gracioso* or two to liven up the play.[32] Critics have seen in Moratín's gleefully tearful response ("You are a good man, Espejo, study your role, study it well, and I will accept the responsibility for all the rest") a kind nobility, although it more clearly reveals an arrogantly patronizing attitude where aesthetics and art were concerned. Yet the company was calmed and the show went on to mixed reviews and conflicting future assessments of its success. Not wrongly, it has been considered the zenith of Spanish Neoclassical theater.

Financially, success was nonexistent. Moratín never had very much money, living off his meager salary and in very modest surroundings. Ramón de la Cruz had held his poverty up to public ridicule in 1764, satirizing his appearance and his ragged clothing. He practiced law now and again, much to his dislike, although Mesonero writes that he was generally sought out as a lawyer.[33] A month after *Hormesinda's* debut he and his wife made up their will, declaring themselves paupers and asking the local parish to bury them when the time came with funds from charity in the place where other paupers were laid to rest. They left "everything" to Leandro. Bernascone stood as witness.

So it was most likely for need of a job that Nicolás entered the competition for the Chair in Poetics at San Isidro, which opened at the end of that year.[34] There had been an earlier competition, in 1768, in which Ayala, Gómez Ortega, and another future member of the San Sebastián Inn tertulia, Juan Bautista Muñoz, had participated, but no permanent selection was made. The king asked Gómez Ortega to be a judge for the 1770 convocation, along with another of Moratín's intimates, Cerdá. It was all very chummy, and Moratín, who had fame as a poet as well as almost a decade of experience in the literary field, expected to be named to the post. Perhaps he became sloppy as a result, because it is surprising that a skilled poet with a strong Latin background would produce a poem and a translation which did not even merit an honorable mention from the judges. Dated December 4, 1770, the "Oda. Al descubrimiento del antiguo Herculano y publicación de estos preciosos monumentos a expensas de laliberalidad del Rey Nuestro Señor'' (Ode. To the Discovery of Ancient Herculaneum and the Publication of These Precious Monuments at the Expense of the Generosity of the King) continued neither the worst nor the best of Moratín's verse. His explanation of it in front of the panel of judges was better, carried out ''with clarity and a knowledge of Latin poets and those of other languages.''[35] Another exercise in translation yielded similar results, plus the interesting discovery that Moratín, whose poems often brimmed with erudite references, chose to forego all grammatical, rhetorical, and mythological notes. Indeed, something was wrong; he came in fourth, far behind Ayala. Leandro tried to embellish the results of his father's work by claiming that he and Ayala were the ''two most outstanding''[36] competitors, but as happened many times with Leandro, love shaded the truth. Here, too, Leandro affectionately quotes his father's remarks to Ayala, hoping to show the former's generosity of spirit, but in fact again showing Nicolás's patronizing arrogance. The words suggest that Moratín believed that Ayala, who was a past student of the Jesuits, would win as a result of that connection, conveniently passing over the fact that he, too, studied with the famous and recently expelled clerical group: ''Do not doubt, Ayala, that the Poetry Chair will be yours....You have been a disciple, an assistant, and a novice of the Jesuits: all of their admirers will now be yours, and I, the first among them, will applaud a selection which is going to fall upon a truly worthy individual and friend.''[37] Yet they did remain friends, a friendship which at this point was perhaps based on a creative antagonism more than on a warm amicability.

Nicolás was still unemployed, or underemployed at least. As Leandro remembers it, he was too proud to beg favors from his well-placed friends, so the financial burdens of supporting a house, a family, and his son's education forced him to turn again, reluctantly, to law. He hated it. As early as the fourth installment of the *Poet* he wrote, ''And finally, I renounced / The predatory craft of law; / I do not wish knowledge which / Offends the poor and saves the rich'' (*Poet,* IV; BAE, 18). He would dedicate himself to ''loftier studies.'' He brushed up on forensic matters and apprenticed himself to a lawyer friend in order to meet the requirements of membership in the bar, which was granted in 1772. Leandro suggests that he could have become rich plying his new trade but that his ethical scruples forced him to care more about morality than money; being right and obtaining justice were apparently two entire different matters. So this failed as well, since he hated the contradictions and machinations of the legal profession. He did get some work as a lawyer to the Royal Council, an association which he kept up at least through 1778.

Nicolás did receive a wage as soon as he took over Ayala's teaching position toward the end of 1773, and he continued in this work until his own death. When he did recover the Chair, he commemorated the occurrence with a poem, still unpublished today, written in the Pindaric tradition,[38] in which he celebrates the goals of the school "since today's tender youth anxiously / Aspire to the prize" of Poetry. He willingly accepts the laurel wreath of his new position, and promises to "sing forth" in service to his country. He encourages his students to do the same. He also received some payments from his job as government censor during this period. So they lived, if not well, and they saved nothing. When Nicolás died, his widow and son were left in desperate straits, forced to petition the government for money to cover the cost of his funeral.[39] Herein lie the seeds of Leandro's obsession with financial details, amply documented in his diary and in his letters.[40] Was this bid for money merely a pose, a formality undertaken first by Nicolás to avoid taxes and later by his son to squeeze a few *reales* out of the government? It is possible, since the *Diary* gives evidence of income received in the two years before Nicolás's death. But 300 *reales* per month, 3,600 per year, was not a lot of money. Jovellanos, in 1795, called 3,300 "a misery,"[41] and even Leandro was earning 1,500 for just three months' work in 1782.[42] The 29,000 Leandro finally began earning as secretary of Interpretation of Languages was considered a good amount. In the 1770s Aranda's director for the Royal Theaters, Luis de Azema y Reynaud, was earning 24,000 *reales* annually, so it is easy to see how Nicolás's 3,600 compared. Yet he spent his money freely in his pursuit of pleasure, he moved frequently (ending up finally in a less than elegant neighborhood), and he had always considered himself to be poor. He wrote of being poor (*Poet,* VI; BAE, 6; *Posthumous Works,* 158-9; BAE, 6), protesting that "my poverty does not bother me" (*Poet,* V; BAE, 38), and Ramón de la Cruz, as we have seen, satirized his shabby state. If he had money, why does his death certificate certify him as poor? If he was not poverty-stricken, neither was he comfortable nor financially secure. On his death certificate we read the word "poor" carefully written into the margin.

IV   *San Sebastián Inn*

The Neoclassical group shared contacts, ideas, and criticisms, and fed upon itself through encouragement and self-enrichment. What it lacked was a focus, a catalyst for coalescence, which would aid it to develop itself even more and to influence literary trends. Even the umbrella of protection provided by the likes of Aranda was too impersonal, too diffuse, and ultimately too ephemeral. So when Aranda's power eclipsed and he was sent off to Paris in 1773, Moratín, while holding back to survey the state of affairs under the new minister not so wholly favorable to Neoclassical ways, encouraged his cohorts to continue meeting on an informal basis. They had for a couple of years been meeting in a back room in the San Sebastián Inn, over in the old "neighborhood of the muses," where Leandro had been born. The room was placed at the disposition of Moratín and company by the Gippini brothers,[43] who enjoyed playing host to compatriots and aficionados of Italian culture. No Frenchmen of note were present but some French poets were read.[44] English writers, too — and, of course, Latin and Greek literature — were studied. But most of all it was Spanish literature which served as a focal point. Perhaps the meetings had gone on even longer, dating back to 1770. All of the participants had been friends for several years and all had shared similar tastes.

It has been universally recognized as one of the most important centers of Neoclassical thought in Spain, following in the tradition of the established academies, including the Academy of Good Taste. Around a chimney Nicolás would gather a host of literary figures, friends old and new. Here in comfort and suitable isolation they read selections from works in progress and discussed them, apparently frankly and with little of the usual animosity and petty jealousy that criticism tends to evoke from literary personalities. Everyone likes to criticize, and no one likes to be criticized, including Moratín, as the nasty polemics of the 1760s and 1770s attest. Yet at the inn, this "almost Academy and semi-Athenaeum,"[45] the men (exclusively so — no women were asked to join) felt comfortable enough to learn from one another. The free-wheeling nature of the discussions had only one guiding tenet, according to Leandro, and that was that the talks be confined to themes concerning the theater, bullfighting, poetry, and "loves." The absence of politics as a topic for discussion is surprising and not entirely believable. It would have been impossible not to consider the fortunes of literary trends that before had been so intimately related to political activities. Surely Aranda's exit and his successor's ideas were discreetly tossed about and most likely lamented, particularly if they were "hiding" in the inn, as Juan Alborg says, to "avoid the possible resentments brought about by the fluctuations in politics."[46]

Moratín acted as the catalyst and the central figure. His pronouncements were accorded considerable weight, and his readings were applauded enthusiastically by the various members of the tertulia: Cadalso, Iriarte, Ayala, Gómez Ortega, Cerdá, Conti, Bernascone, and Signorelli formed the core, with figures such as Guevara, Muñoz, Pineda, Pizzi, and Ríos dropping in to contribute to the activities. This was Neoclassical Madrid, and their productions and positions proved it.

Cadalso read there some of his satirical *Cartas marruecas* (Moroccan Letters), in which he included veiled references to the group, much to their amusement.[47] Moratín had stood by Cadalso during the difficulties he suffered in the past four years — his exile from Madrid and the tragic death of his adored Filis, the same María Ignacia Ibáñez who had brightened the Madrid stage in the leading roles of *Hormesinda* and Cadalso's own *Sancho García* — and their friendship was all the stronger for it. They composed poems for one another, some of which were no doubt read at the tertulia. Cadalso's flatteries of the "divine"[48] Moratín reached disproportionate heights, but they were returned by Nicolás, and the camaraderie of the group was frequently reemphasized. Dalmiro composed and read his "A Venus y Cupido, con motivo de unos nuevos amores" (To Venus and Cupid, Owing to a New Love), to which Moratín responded with his own "A un nuevo amor de Dalmiro" (To a New Love of Dalmiro).[49] Three other poems to Moratín attest to the mutual respect of these two poets. A "Song," a Pindaric ode, and an Anacreontic ode[50] all revealed with typical rhetorical flourish the depth of Cadalso's feelings toward his "divine" friend, whose odes reached such exceptional heights that Ercilla, Herrera, Horace, and Homer are all silenced! Cadalso suggests that he initially felt jealousy toward Moratín's success ("I hated your name"), but was soon seduced by Nicolás's friendly ways and unthreatening devotion to poetic art. Other ties that united them were the delicious times that the foursome Flumisbo-

Dorisa-Dalmiro-Filis spent together, and which both men so often recorded in their poetry. Cadalso considered Moratín the finer poet, but Cadalso added a great deal of spark to the tertulia with his charm, his generosity, and his wit.

Witty as well was Tomás de Iriarte, even though his periodic use of it against Nicolás threatened to subvert the good relations established between the two men. Tomás's uncle, Juan, had been friendly with Moratín for years, and even though Juan was considerably older, he and Moratín shared many similar tastes, most notably their love for the bullfight[51] and the rules of Neoclassical literature. As royal librarian, Juan was in a position to know and to influence younger generations of writers; when Tomás came to Madrid in 1764 his uncle wasted no time in throwing him headlong into the leading literary circles, in which Moratín was prominent. Tomás became a crusading Neoclassicist who provided translations of French plays for the official royal theaters set up by Aranda and headed by the old *Thinker,* Clavijo, and entered into heated polemics with his enemies, most notably Ramón de la Cruz. He joined the tertulia with his brothers, and relished the forum for criticism and expression. He first brought up some of the ideas on music which later appeared in *La Música* to the *tertulianos* (members of the group) and contributed to the careful analysis of style to which they subjected many domestic and foreign productions. Perhaps here is where some of the ideas for his *Fábulas literarias* (Literary Fables) began to take on a clearer focus. Iriarte was working on his translation of Horace's *Poetics,* sections of which he read aloud in that clubby back room. Ironically, when the work was ready for publication in 1777, the Council of Castile submitted it to Moratín, then working as a free-lance censor, who unenthusiastically gave it his seal of approval.[52]

From the Imperial College came Ayala, friend and competitor of Moratín, to read his works and to join in the artistic fun. It was here that he read sections from his work in progress, *La Numancia destruida* (Numancia Destroyed), written at the inspiration of Moratín's original patriotic tragedy of a few years earlier. He subjected it to the criticism of his peers, and apparently listened, too. According to Leandro, Nicolás was instrumental in encouraging Ayala to excise a particularly gory scene in which characters appeared with their arms severed. Signorelli raised some objections also, but Ayala ignored those, and Signorelli was content to publish his reservations in the *Storia critica dei teatri* (A Critical History of the Theater), which came out in 1777. Ayala was one of the most active writers in the group, and he presented to them another tragedy, *Abidis,* along with several sections from his ongoing biographical studies of Spanish heroes, the *Vidas de españoles ilustres* (Lives of Illustrious Spaniards).[53]

Signorelli all along had been collecting materials for a history of Spanish drama and discussing his knowledge with Moratín. The tertulia provided a wider forum for speculation and commentary. As an expert on European theater, Signorelli contributed enormously to the erudite discussions while picking up interesting bits and pieces of information, which he stored away for future use. He was particularly useful in dispersing the Neoclassicists' distaste for the popular Ramón de la Cruz and they were gleeful when his attacks reached print in the 1777 volume.[54] The men, especially Nicolás, also schooled Signorelli in the intricacies of Spanish drama and saw to it that the Italian understood the special genius of Lope, Calderón, Tirso, Moreto, and others. Signorelli learned well. Moratín's admiration for his Italian friend appeared in an ode in which he praised the monumental task undertaken by Signorelli, a praise shared by Leandro, who became his close friend in subsequent years. Signorelli even translated Leandro's plays *El viejo y la niña* (The Old Man and the Girl) and *El sí de las niñas* (When a Girl Says Yes) into his native language.

Conti, four years younger than Moratín, added a cosmopolitan poetic dimension to the proceedings by discussing his translations of Garcilaso and other Spanish poets. He had been in Madrid since 1765 and was living in the same building as the Moratín and Bernascone families (he was the latter's son-in-law), as a consequence of which he, Bernascone, and Moratín were the closest of friends. There was a great cross-fertilization of ideas among the three which added impetus to the discussions at the inn. According to another friend, Casimiro Gómez Ortega, "They cultivated their talents with esteem and mutual advantage and [Conti] appreciated the love and knowledge which [Moratín] gave him of our poets."[55] Nicolás contributed a couple of sonnets and odes to his friend's famous 1771 edition of Garcilaso's first *Eclogue,* and Gómez Ortega wrote a prologue to it.[56] His translations earned him Menéndez Pelayo's commendation as the principal Italian Hispanist of the eighteenth century,[57] as well as considerable notoriety in his own time. He was gifted with an analytical mind, which he applied evenly to his judgments of Spanish Renaissance poets. Moratín was charmed and instructed by him.

Ignacio Bernascone shared most of Moratín's views, which he publicized whenever he could. It was he who had written the fiery prologue to the printed version of *Hormesinda,* in which he attacked, among other things, the theater of Ramón de la Cruz. His own contributions do not seem to be as substantial as those of his housemates and friends, although his scholarly love for the men and topics which stimulated the others always made him a welcome member of this erudite gathering. He did play a pivotal role in the transmission of the elder Moratín's works down to us, according to the dubious testimony of Leandro: Nicolás was apparently preparing a manuscript version of his complete works when his final illness struck in 1780. Several months before he died he handed his materials over to Bernascone, or so says Leandro, who passed them on to the son. Leandro published them with new corrections in 1821.[58] There is reason to disbelieve Leandro's version of the tale, as we shall see later.

The corpulant Casimiro Gómez Ortega — mockingly called "Botelio" by Juan Pablo Forner — held the distinction of being recognized as his country's leading botanist. As a sidelight he cultivated Latin poetry, and his school-day contacts with Conti in Bologna from 1761 drew him into the San Sebastián circle. Menéndez Pelayo believes that Ortega was chiefly responsible for Conti's interest and refinement in the realm of Spanish letters, encouraging him to undertake his important translations.[59] He contributed a flattering poem to the printed version of *Hormesinda* and much later translated Leandro's lament on the death of Meléndez Valdés into Latin. Just three years Nicolás's junior, he was an enormously cultured man who traveled widely, inspecting botanical specimens in France, England, Holland, and Italy. He was appointed to the first chair in the newly formed Royal Botanical Gardens (1771). He was a prolific author of botanical and geographical treatises, writing with equal ease in Spanish or in Latin; he often translated current books on the physical sciences from French and English. He was at the height of his activity and glory during the years he frequented the inn, and brought to the discussions a worldliness and scientific perspective, particularly in drawing his friends' attention to the latest discoveries of the natural sciences. He had wider contacts as well through his memberships in societies ranging from the Royal Medical Academy, the Royal Academy of History, and the Royal Economic Society of Madrid to academies in London, Paris, and Florence.[60] His interests stimulated Moratín's along similar lines and encouraged him to join the Economic Society, which was established in Madrid in 1776.

There were others who came to these amicable gatherings. Francisco Cerdá y Rico was a fellow lawyer of Moratín's who shared the latter's lukewarm interest in his profession. He was much more drawn to the works of past Spanish authors he discovered on the shelves of the Royal Library, where he worked, and he set out to publish as many of those forgotten works as he could. The results were impressive editions of works by Cervantes de Salazar, Lope de Vega, Juan de Moncada, Alfonso el Sabio, Villaviciosa, Gil Polo, Fray Luis de León, Jorge Manrique, and others. Moratín was delighted with the endeavor, which addressed itself to his earlier complaint that many Spanish authors were difficult to locate or expensive to buy. Juan Bautista Muñoz, a theological philosopher, carried the enlightened banner of Feijoo in fighting superstitions and sloppy thinking. He shared Moratín's rabid hatred of scholasticism, vowing to have it banished from university classrooms; also like Moratín he exhorted youth to study select Spanish authors, reading to the tertulia selections from Fray Luis de Granada. But it was his *Historia del Nuevo Mundo* (History of the New World) that earned him greatest recognition. Mariano Pizzi, Arabic language teacher and colleague of Ayala at the Imperial College, had also worked in the Royal Library along with Juan de Iriarte, Cerdá, and so many others. Pizzi was a source of fascinating information on Arabic life, the kind of colorful details which Moratín loved and which he so dashingly included in some of his poems, most notably the well-known "Fiesta de toros en Madrid" (Bullfight Festival in Madrid). It is not unlikely that Moratín's knowledge of Arabic customs, dress, social relationships, and place names came directly from Pizzi.[61]

Vicente de los Ríos was busy preparing an edition of Villegas's poetry, which he read to the group as it progressed; it sparked interest in Cadalso, a fellow soldier, who asked Moratín about it from Salamanca in late 1773.[62] De los Ríos was also working on a study of Cervantes, selections of which he read at both the tertulia and at the Royal Academy of the Language, to which he was elected in early 1773; this prompted his biography and study of the great novelist, which prefaces the Academy's 1780 edition of *Don Quijote*. José de Guevara, secretary of the Academy of History and future colleague of Moratín and Gómez Ortega at the Royal Economic Society, contributed his, as Cotarelo puts it, puffed-up vanity and rantings on literary matters. Antonio de Pineda, a young military man with interests in literature and the natural sciences, often joined his acquaintances, in particular Gómez Ortega, whom he frequently accompanied on botanical field trips. Professor Catena includes two other individuals in the gatherings at the inn: an enlightened serviceman, Captain Enrique Ramos (brought in by Cadalso and Ríos?) and a certain Manual Alcázar, of whom nothing is known.[63]

It has been said that Juan López Sedano joined in the meetings, but the nature of his relations with the group would suggest that he was more talked about than with. To hear Leandro tell it,[64] the *tertulianos* read López Sedano's *Parnaso español* (Spanish Parnassus), but did not necessarily agree with the emphasis or presentation of the works. So Moratín and Ayala schemed to write a critique entitled *Reflexiones críticas dirigidas al colector de el Parnaso, don Juan López Sedano* (Critical Reflections Directed to the Collector of the Parnassus, Juan López Sedano), which the group liked and encouraged the pair to publish. Moratín, however, thought better of it, feeling that López Sedano would be so chastened with the criticism that he would cease his efforts completely, defeating the purpose of the criticism which was to "correct" rather than silence him. Besides, the publisher, Antonio de Sancha, was a mutual friend and they saw no need to hurt him unnecessarily. The whole episode did not stop Sedano from attacking other members of the San Sebastián group — Iriarte and Ríos — in a later volume of the Parnassus and thereby provoking the very polemic Moratín had wanted to avoid.

As to his father's actual contribution to the group's activities, other than acting as a master critic and *éminence grise,* Leandro is less forthright. Nicolás was not working on any specific project during this period but he was still writing poetry. In fact we can imagine the twitters occasioned by readings from his scabrous poem *El arte de las putas* (The Whores' Art), composed in 1771 or 1772. Also, baiting Ramón de la Cruz was still one of the Neoclassicists' favorite pastimes, and Cotarelo suggests that Nicolás was the author of an earlier-composed critical attack on him entitled *Examen imparcial de las Labradoras* (An Impartial Examination of "The Working Women").[65]

How important was the tertulia in the San Sebastián Inn? What real impact did it exert upon the direction of Spanish letters? The group met on a somewhat regular basis from 1770 or 1771; all the members were located in close-knit Madrid, all had known one another for some years, and all shared similar interests. It is not true that they met only following Aranda's fall: there would have been no time for meetings since the gradual dissolution of the tertulia as a formal entity came in 1773, when Cadalso received orders transferring him to Salamanca (May); Ayala became ill again (October); Conti returned to Italy upon hearing of his father's death; and Iriarte spent increasingly more time outside Madrid at the royal theater sites. The tertulia was, then, surprisingly shortlived. Its impact was highly concentrated because of the positions of influence held by individual members: they were a diverse group of poets and dramatists, scholars and critics, professors, publishers, soldiers, scientists, Arabists, philosophers, and historians, but they had one purpose in common. They recognized a collapse of literary taste in Spain and felt obligated to try to stem the tide of "corrupt" literature in their country. As models they chose old Spanish masters as well as examples from foreign literatures. Of those foreign literatures Menéndez Pelayo is correct to emphasize the Italian influences. Leandro himself says that they read Italian poets like the contemporaries Carlo Innocenzo Frugoni, whose Anacreontic odes were impressive to Moratín and Cadalso, and Vincenzo Filicaia, author of patriotic epics. They enjoyed the Renaissance love sonnets of Gabriello Chiabrera. Favorites, of course, were Petrarch, Tasso, and Ariosto, and Leandro provides anecdotes to highlight his father's preference for these individuals. They did study French poetry, sparingly, and French poetics in Boileau's *L'Art poétique*. Most likely, notwithstanding Leandro's claim to the contrary, they pored over Luzán's *Poetics* as well (Nicolás had appealed to its authority in an earlier work). They were a highly self-conscious lot, aware of their sophisticated goals and directly involved with reform. They constituted an entire intellectual network whose web encompassed academies, schools, and salons all over town. Several were members of the Academies of History and of the Language; they belonged to the Academy of San Fernando; Ayala taught at San Isidro and later became an official drama censor; Ortega took the message back to the botanical school; Iriarte shouted a lot, determined to have his say in the definition of "good taste"; Cadalso carried the aims of the group with him to Salamanca, where he made friends with young poets there (González, Iglesias de la Casa, Meléndez Valdés).[66]

The Madrid tertulia was international in scope, cosmopolitan in outlook. Moratín himself enjoyed the respect of highly placed individuals. Among his friends or protectors he could count the king's son Gabriel; Count Campomanes; the ambassadors from Italy and France; the Duke and Duchess of Arcos; the enormously respected Duke and Duchess of Medinasidonia; minister Eugenio Llaguno; Aranda, of course; and others. The meetings, as we note from the strictly middle-class membership, were not aristocratic playthings, even if they did enjoy the admiration of the social elite. But those contacts were extremely important, for when Moratín talked, his noble friends listened, and often echoed many of his views; and when they talked, everyone listened, particularly if those views were reinforced by Carlos III or his emissaries. And what they were listening to was a new enthusiasm for Latin, Greek, Italian, French, English, and especially Spanish authors, which formed a body of literary ideas that was to traverse geographical and temporal boundaries. It is easy to see the close working relations they had established among themselves, this one writing a poem for that one, criticizing a work here, contributing a prologue there, translating some pieces, listening, talking, sharing. Alborg notes that the tertulia was the force most responsible for the change of ideas and aesthetic impulses which took place during Carlos III's reign (1759–89), while Cotarelo discusses the flurry of pamphlets and incidental publications released by lesser authors, which reflected the group's ideas and influenced public opinion.[67]

It was, in short, "the most distinguished tertulia of the eighteenth century,"[68] and Leandro was sometimes there. Even though the precocious lad was only eleven or twelve years old at the time, he often listened to the intellectual rantings of the men involved. They left a lasting impression on him. Most of the men were his father's age or slightly younger, and most continued their literary activities after the eclipse of the tertulia, which gave Leandro cause to continue the friendships first established at the inn. Several became his lifelong friends.

V Poems, Plays, and Plants

Ayala's illnesses and his retirements to Grazalema provided Moratín with the opportunity to recover a lost goal when he was named to replace his friend as Professor of Poetics at the prestigious Imperial College. He kept busy preparing classes, writing poetry, and trying his best to influence a younger generation of scholars. His teaching techniques were Socratic — calm conversation and informed questions balanced with example and, of course, discussions of the rules of art. For years he had been bitterly critical of the country's educational system, even to the extent of refusing to let his son automatically be placed in the hands of either the State or the Church. As far as the teaching of poetry was concerned, he planted hints of what his own goals would be as early as the second *Reproach,* where he wrote:

> . . . ignorant people should realize that, in matters that they do not understand, they are not capable of making decisions; and so long as those who have studied things are speaking, the rest should observe a profound silence. This is the shame of poetry, that has as many critics as listeners, when the lowest and most mechanical trade declines authority and only lets itself be governed by those who call themselves teachers, whose skills, for the most part, consist merely in possessing some tools.[69]

He sought to continue what in fact had been his whole life's occupation, that is, to teach the principles of "good taste." As Leandro remembered it, "He had his students use not memory but understanding; he had them reason more than learn"[70] and he shunned the parrotlike repetition of memorized question-and-answer pedagogy which so often passed for teaching. When he attended public ceremonies where such techniques were in evidence he responded to his students like this: "Here you have a band of magpies and thrushes who are saying things they do not understand. Whoever of you wishes to be pedantic and fatuous, a superficial scholar and a daring talker, come to these classrooms and the teacher will show you how to do it." More in keeping with his own focus is the answer he provided for a student who solicited his advice on which poets and which nations he should study. Nicolás's famous response, "Greeks and Spaniards, Latins and Spaniards, Italians and Spaniards, French and Spaniards, English and Spaniards," amply documents his own cosmopolitan beliefs and shows that he never strayed far from his own country's literary heritage.

When a contingent of Arabs attempted to lay siege to Melilla, the Spanish possession in Africa, the city resisted with a courage and stamina reminiscent of that of Numancia centuries earlier. Ayala was preparing to publish his heroic tragedy on Numancia; and Moratín, captivated by the nobility of the residents of Melilla, began to plan his own work on the theme of community resistance to oppression. He read in the *Gaceta de Madrid* in March and April of 1775 that the situation looked promising for the defending Spanish Christians, and his drama took shape. With amazing speed (six hours spread over three evenings) he composed his play which, according to Leandro, was well received by his longtime patron the Duke of Medinasidonia, and even by the king himself. Moratín might at last have an all-out success. But the king advised against a precipitous staging of the play that June, since he was at that very moment planning a full-scale attack on troubled North Africa, and he was against any before-the-fact backslapping. It proved to be a wise decision. In July the Spanish fleet was brutally defeated in Algiers, and everyone involved with *La defensa de Melilla* (The Defense of Melilla) could have been caught shamefully redfaced.[71] Moratín may have destroyed this work in bitter disappointment; no copies exist today and we know nothing about it.

Patriotic resistance against any odds reappeared as the primary subject in another tragedy written two years later. In 1777 *Guzmán el Bueno* (Guzmán the Brave) was presented to one of Guzmán's real descendants, the same Duke of Medinasidonia. Moratín's established tradition of plays written but not staged remained intact; this work was his last play. For a year or so he had been involved in nontheatrical endeavors and increasing his poetic activities. His prose and verse collection was once again announced to the readers of the *Gaceta* in June of that year. July 25, 1776, is the date signed on his treatise "Carta histórica sobre el origen y progresos de las fiestas de toros en España" (Historical Letter Concerning the Origin and Advances of the Bullfight in Spain). The title is self-explanatory and the contents demonstrate Moratín's longtime love affair with the Spanish national sport. The subject fascinated him from childhood and became an integral part of several of his best-known works, including the still popular "Fiesta de toros en Madrid."

One of the dominant interests of the last four years of his life was the newly formed Royal Economic Society of Madrid. The society was founded in 1776. Moratín was passionately interested in this latest practical application of enlightened scientific thought. He actively sought membership by composing a short dissertation in response to the society's open search for a solution to the problem of how to stimulate the country's agricultural production without adversely affecting the livestock industry. The question was posed publicly in the end of 1776, and Moratín's ideas were set down in a matter of days. A prize of 1,500 *reales* (nearly half his yearly salary) was offered for the best ideas; Moratín's timidity, or perhaps his reticence to be humiliated by a "loss" in the competition, persuaded him to hand it in under the name of Rafael Fernández; it took the society a few months to discover to whom it belonged. Sixteen others were entered, several of which bested his "Memoria sobre los medios de fomentar la agricultura en España, sin perjuicios de la cría de ganados" (Dissertation on How to Improve Agriculture in Spain Without Harming the Raising of Livestock), although his was considered good enough to earn him permanent membership in the society's agricultural section by June 1777.

The piece, minus a few satirical barbs, which "shouldn't be included," was selected for printing in the first volume of the society's *Memoirs*. In it, Moratín demonstrated a positive attitude toward Spain's abilities to cure her agricultural problems, and a disdain for his country's critics, particularly for those who thought Spaniards lazy or unable to establish a viable agricultural base. While admitting to the sorry state of Spanish agriculture, he forcefully states that it is not a result of ignorance, apathy, or poor techniques on the part of the farmers. His reasoning is not wholly supported by fact since he overemphasizes what was a recognized problem — underpopulation. In his view, an increase in population would cure all agricultural ills, and the treatise details methods to do so. Nor does he stop there. He claims that a population growth will result in better production in all economic endeavors, including industry, trade, manufacturing, and even the arts. The interest in this discourse, if we can get past an obviously simplistic view of the Spanish economy, resides in his call for land reform, a subject of the greatest urgency which is still troublesome.

From then on he became an indefatigable supporter of the society's goals. He assiduously attended the meetings[72] (except when he would retire to his mother's family lands in Pastrana, which he had been doing during the summer for years, and even then he often carried on grain-growing experiments for the society[73]), and he frequently accepted assignments to review agricultural dissertations written by other members, prepare works for publication, study special problems, and read his own poems during the annual ceremonies for the schools run by the organization. Some of those assignments reveal the patterns of Moratín's interests in the last years of his life. He read or worked on statements concerning general agricultural techniques, grain production, new scientific experiments, the planting of trees, the usefulness of the Kermes insect, the propagation of mulberry and olive trees, and worker guilds.

He volunteered for an eight-man commission which met thrice weekly to study questions sent in from the provinces which could not properly be addressed in the regular Tuesday meetings. He was active as a decision-maker, a literary censor, whose task it was to report back to the society on the merits of different items presented for publication;[74] not all were approved. He was on a four-man commission charged with preparing the *Memoirs* for publication; Antonio de Sancha was the publisher and he brought out the first volume in 1780.[75] Moratín's own dissertation was excerpted in the *Gaceta,* which discussed the *Memoirs* on June 27, 1780, just a few weeks after his death. Moratín worked hard on the *Memoirs,* giving progress reports to the society every month or two, beginning in early 1778. There were several occasions when he was asked to function as the substitute secretary (September 19 and 26, 1778), and to conduct the routine business of reading minutes, reports, and taking notes. At times he was asked to write funeral statements in honor of departed members, and of course his poems praising the industriousness of the schoolgirls were distributed. Moratín was present to work on Cabarrús's request for an increase of trees in the environs of Madrid (he was appointed to a special commission to report on the matter; the report was given on February 9, 1779, but it merely called for new reports and further study). His diary reveals that he had frequent contact with Cabarrús, the Duke of Frías, and Barberán during the period toward the end of 1778 when they worked on their assignments together.

He obviously was concerned with the well-being of Spanish society and if this forum was new to him his desires for reform were not. His inaugural speech, given before the body on Saturday, June 21, 1777, emphasized his attraction to the "patriots" who comprised the membership, and to the service which they rendered to the nation:

Besides the honor and instructive advantages which I receive, I also am able to serve the nation with my scant intelligence. I see before me so many wise men who will constantly animate my intelligence, admiration, and respect: these men who out of love for their country, without other interest, and at great cost to themselves, have founded this Royal Economic Society of Madrid. This establishment is capable of bringing honor, by itself, to a century, a nation, and a government.[76]

Perhaps more important, he answers those foreign critics who would make Spain out to be a useless and sterile country. This note of strong patriotism is a salient feature in many of his works.

One week later he presented to the body a more detailed and startlingly liberal defense of workers' rights, in which he attempted to clarify one of the principal causes of low productivity: the "wicked treatment" given to trade apprentices. "The life of these unfortunate individuals is the most bitter and unhappy that can be imagined...their masters treat them with extreme cruelty and contempt, using them worse than slaves or beasts...they despise them, teach them nothing...they punish them cruelly, not only the masters, but mistresses, too, and their children, relatives, neighbors, and servants."[77] The eighteenth-century demands for the rights of the individual and Rousseau's plea for humane social treatment for all men found a forceful and eloquent spokesman in Moratín, and Moratín found an audience for the most impassioned speech he ever made. He pleaded for the society to take charge of the education of these trade apprentices, just as it had done for the girls in the spinning and weaving trades.

The group's censor, Nicolás's old friend José de Guevara, approved the piece for inclusion in the society's archives, and, although the plans were not brought to fruition, it was still being discussed a year later. The enlightened thinker's belief that social good would spring from rational study and diligent application of hard work once again became evident in Moratín. "Moratín believed that there he could be usefully occupied, and that there he could fulfill the desire he always had to see his nation less backward, more industrious, less ignorant, and less satisfied with that ignorance."[78] He was not alone. Many of his friends were or were to become members; the membership rolls were a Who's Who of the Madrid power structure: Ortega, Ayala, Guevara, Bernardo Iriarte, the painter Mengs, Campomanes, Pignatelli, Medinasidonia, Arcos, Grimaldi, a host of other nobles and ecclesiastical authorities, and, later, Jovellanos (admitted September 26, 1778), whose "Informe sobre la ley agraria" (Report on the

Agrarian Law) was no doubt one of the society's most important accomplishments. The society received the full support of the king. Ayala, feeling better by 1777, was welcomed back into it in September, and he joined Moratín at several meetings that fall.[79] Moratín remained intimately involved with the society until his death.

Moratín was not a joiner. There were few organizations to which he belonged. But he did participate actively in at least two: the Economic Society, and the Arcadians of Rome, who asked him to become a member in the early 1760s. This poetic "club" dedicated itself to the study, production, and dissemination of Classical and Neoclassical poetic ideals. All of the members were given pastoral or Classical pseudonyms. The unwieldy name fastened upon Moratín was used throughout his career, starting from his very first publication of poetic significance — *The Madrilenian Poet* — whose title page presented its author as Moratín, "known among the Arcadians of Rome as Flumisbo Thermodonciaco."[80] He may have been a member of the Latin Academy of Madrid.[81] He was never asked to affiliate with the Royal Spanish Academy of the Language, even though several of his close friends had achieved that honor. In Leandro's mind, his father's failure to do so was due to his disdain for that group and to his belief that literary merit was not the sole price for admission. Nicolás was probably right, but his comments, as quoted by his son, sound somewhat like sour grapes. After all, he himself was the recipient of special favors and patronage not always intimately linked with artistic merit. He did not always feel this way. In fact, in the first installment of the *Reproaches* he held the academy in high esteem. His complaint was that the various academies were not sufficiently respected as arbiters of good taste: "...It is not the members of the Spanish Academy, nor of the Academies of Sciences at London or Paris, nor of the Arcadians of Rome, but actors, and even worse poetasters, or versifying *sainete*-writers and *entremés*-scribblers, who run around with acting companies: these people are the judges poetry has in Spain."[82] In the third *Reproach* he repeats the idea that only these academies have the true right to censure poetry. We can speculate that Moratín attacked the academy as it became evident that he would not be asked to join it (neither was Tomás de Iriarte), although by the end of the nineteenth century the academy recognized Moratín's works as models for the use of the language. He took some swipes at the body in his *The Whores' Art,* by vaguely comparing that august group of intellectuals to a bordello, presumably suggesting that the members prostituted their art for more immediate and tangible rewards.[83] Leandro quotes him as writing: "Solid merit ought to find the road open to the academical chair...not favors and interest."[84] The academy's reasons for excluding him are not entirely understandable.

His hostility toward the academy was increased by the "Cortés" incident of 1777–78. The academy decided to stimulate poetic activity by convoking competitions, the winners of which would receive prizes, public recognition from the academy, and publication of the winning poems at the academy's expense. Moratín wrote and handed in a work entitled "Las naves de Cortés destruidas" (Cortés's Ships Destroyed). This epic poem seemed destined to win; Moratín was after all one of the country's leading poets and now professor of poetry. The academy's opinion of it was less than favorable, and the prize went to an unknown, José Vaca de Guzmán. Ironically, just months earlier in his inaugural address to the Economic Society, he voiced his belief that the accomplishments of the society would be such that the "delicate pens" of other "noble institutions" would be stimulated along worthy lines, no longer bothering with "trivial and sad themes of battles, fires, death, destruction, and disorder."[85] He was not unused to failure. His 1763 poem on the military defense of Havana for the Royal Society of San Fernando and the Latin poems he wrote for the 1770 Imperial College poetics chair were other examples, but he was disappointed enough to stay out of future competitions and to withhold publication of the poem. He was somewhat vindicated when Leandro, hidden behind the anagrammatical pseudonym of Efrén de Lardnaz y Morante[86] and only nineteen years old, walked off with the academy's honorable mention in 1779. Nicolás's joy in his son's success is touchingly recorded by Leandro's friend Silvela.[87]

By January 1780, Moratín was seriously ill. The scrawlings in his diary[88] became weaker and appeared less frequently, and his participation in the Economic Society stopped completely. His financial situation had not improved much, although he did make a living with intermittent payments from the Imperial College; intermittent because Ayala had returned in late 1777 and had accepted periodic duties at the school. When Nicolás died, the tables were turned, and Ayala became the poetry master once again, a governmental literary censor (as Nicolás had been[89]), and even the man selected to read the annual poem at the Economic Society's year-end ceremonies. Ayala personally granted the permission for the 1785 publication of the "Cortés's Ships" poem. Leandro in 1821 wrote that his family did not "suffer the anguish of poverty,"[90] apparently forgetting that they were forced to move to an old place down in the Cava Baja on May 1,[91] just ten days before his father's death. He also chose not to remember the struggles which he and his mother encountered in trying to recover the partial salary owed to his father.[92] Or that his mother was in desperate need of money the very day he died ("the death of her husband leaves her in the greatest affliction and need"[93]). Or that Isidora solicited alms from the government to help pay for the funeral. Or that Nicolás was buried a pauper. Or, that he was buried "in secret." Leandro worked hard to support his mother, and evidence has been published which documents his own financial sources during this period of transition,[94] some of it in meager royalties earned from the sale of *Hormesinda*.

What caused Moratín's early death? We do not know the exact cause. In his diary he cryptically writes that he suffered periodic attacks of gout. Gout is a hereditary disease which usually strikes the male, yet to our knowledge neither his father nor his grandfather suffered from it, and both lived relatively long lives (his father was still alive as late as 1776). Besides, gout was rarely fatal and attacks of it that would have been serious enough to produce secondary death by, say, kidney failure would have made it impossible for him to participate in anything or to move to another house. Gout was also a disease of the wealthy and the overweight, those who could afford to indulge in rich living, and nothing suggests that Moratín was either wealthy or overweight, although he could — and did — participate in periods of relatively hedonistic living. Therefore perhaps we need to look elsewhere for the cause of his death.

We know that Moratín had a weakness for Madrid's ladies of the night, and he did not enjoy a particularly close relationship with his wife. The overriding fear in his poem *The Whores' Art* is that of contracting venereal disease, which he writes about passionately and knowledgeably. Why was he given a secret burial? Why did he die so young? Did he, in fact, die of the "Gallic plague" (as he calls it), syphilis? Had he contracted the disease young, it is a medical possibility that it would have advanced sufficiently to cause joint discomfort (similar to gout) and ultimate failure of the heart's aortic vein — that is, a death-producing situation. Why does he talk of gout and diet in the diary? First, it would seem unlikely that he would be so candid as to write anything like "April 20. I have V.D." — even in the multilingual shorthand that he used in the book. Second, and more significantly, the Oxford English Dictionary lists gout as a slang euphemism used "in names for the venereal disease." Was this fact being hidden?

Leandro's passionless lament on Nicolás's death does not do justice to the love he had for his father. Written in 1780, the verses "To the Memory of Nicolás Fernández de Moratín"[95] reveal a distanced respect rather than a true appreciation of his father's contribution to the direction of his life; that appreciation would come later as he reconstructed his father's place in Spanish letters for the 1821 *Posthumous Works*. That Leandro was influenced by his father cannot be doubted. Nicolás's friends, his library, his ideals, his aspirations, and his direction became Leandro's. A minor talent would have smothered under the weight of such a brilliant burden: Leandro's genius was such that he was able to synthesize that experience and distill it into some of Spain's greatest literary achievements. Nicolás's example was not easily forgotten. The opening of *When a Girl Says Yes* in Zaragoza in 1806 prompted one of Nicolás's former students to jot a pair of letters to Leandro in which he recalled the "infinite number of lessons, as much on conduct as on poetry, which I received" from Moratín;[96] the father's former student played the lead role in the son's most brilliant play. Juan Nicasio Gallego was not above accusing Leandro of outright plagiarism,[97] while René Andioc perceptively notes certain similarities between Nicolás's Lucretia and the comic female in *The Old Man and the Girl*.[98] Menéndez Pelayo saw echoes of the San Sebastián Inn in Leandro's *The New Comedy or the Café,* and the influence is not always considered favorable, as the harsh words of Azorín demonstrate.[99] More intriguingly, the lines of influence often blur or run backward: Leandro, known to be a detailed polisher of his own works, rewrote many of his father's pieces before publishing them, as we shall see in later chapters.

Nicolás Fernández de Moratín was forty-two years old when he died on May 11, 1780.

CHAPTER 2

Attack and Defend

NEOCLASSICISM quite literally was a new Classicism. As this new Classicism developed in Spain, it became bivalent, encompassing two seemingly disparate elements: rejection and rediscovery. The rejection was of the extravagance of the baroque Golden Age, while the rediscovery centered upon Classical and Renaissance literary masters. The matter is not as clear-cut as some would have us believe. Most of the Spanish Neoclassicists rejected much of the tortured baroque style, searching instead for a clearer, simpler style in which to express their ideas. But many of them also learned from their Golden Age ancestors and integrated bits and pieces of that earlier style into their own productions. Likewise, the rediscovery of the authors of Classical antiquity (or perhaps we should say reemphasis of their importance) and of European Renaissance writers was not a phenomenon that produced a band of rigid Spanish Neoclassicists all marching to the same drummer. Yet one thing did unite them, and that was the attempt to achieve, in their theoretical writing as well as in their poetic and dramatic creations, that certain ill-defined commodity that they came to call "good taste."

"Good taste" included as much as it excluded. "Good taste" was artifice, imitation, reserve, decorum, polish; it was not hyperbole, hyperbaton, or conceit. It led to good manners, healthful customs, and instructive habits. It established a hierarchy of human activity. It followed the models and the rules of art. It chose to lead and to form the tastes of the people, not to follow them. It was elitist.

Thematically, Neoclassicism was also bivalent, adopting both a pastoral and a scientific (enlightened) stance. In poetry, this meant recourse to Homer, Anacreon, Tasso, etc.; in drama, it was the Classical form of Terence and Plautus combined with elements rediscovered by the French Neoclassicists of the seventeenth century.

The theories, as they developed in Spain, were given support by treatises such as those of Aristotle and, more recently, Boileau's *L'Art poétique*. But in connection with Spanish Neoclassicism we must consider an element that is of crucial importance to our understanding of it: nationalism. Even Ignacio de Luzán, whose 1737 *Arte poética* is considered one of the key works in Spanish Neoclassicism, used more Spanish sources than he is generally given credit for.[1] Moratín's fervent patriotism will be discussed in later chapters. Spain awakened slowly to Neoclassical ideals. During the second quarter of the eighteenth century men like Luzán, Juan de Iriarte, Velázquez, Montiano, and Nasarre developed ideas that settled upon Moratín easily. Raised in an atmosphere much more open to international influences — it is fair to recognize that the French and Italians preceded the Spanish in the development of literary Neoclassicism — Moratín slowly came to believe in the need for literary reform. Once he arrived at that belief he was not slow to act upon it.

Moratín is best remembered as an intolerant firebrand, one of those French-spewing haters of Spain's glorious Golden-Age masters. The characterization is ridiculous and wrong. His critical theories were presented in treatises, prologues to his works, and even integrated into his poetry. In them he attempted to outline his ideas of what was not to be done in order to produce good literature. He used examples to support his positions. He used ridicule and sarcasm to defeat his "enemies." He challenged his oponents to do better, to defy him, to prove him wrong. He exaggerated, shouted, worked hard, and influenced an entire generation of Spanish authors.

I *Lope and Calderón, Literally:* Desengaños al teatro español

Moratín's most important theoretical writing is the series of three short treatises known as the *Desengaños al teatro español* (Reproaches to the Spanish Theater), in which he attacks what he views as the exaggerations of Spanish Golden-Age theater and the frankly dangerous *autos sacramentales*. The pieces were written and published in 1762–63,[2] just after Moratín had composed his plays *La petimetra* and *Lucrecia,* both of which carried prologues. In the *Reproaches* Moratín combines poetry and drama (dramatic poetry), thereby pulling his examples from both genres.

The first sentence of *Reproach 1* contains Moratín's synoptic view of what theater should be: its perfection is important for the nation's honor as well as for the improvement of customs. It also contains evidence of his critical posture — the arrogance of those who are convinced they are right and have a stranglehold on "truth." Or perhaps it was merely the assurance of youth, for he was barely twenty-five when the first *Reproach* appeared. He will not bore us with pedantic affectation, he tells us, but rather use "natural reason," since "he who has it need not force it";[3] whatever goes beyond the borders of what is "natural" is madness and "with this it is all said." These initial thoughts also encompass his frame of reference: the very first authors he evokes for support are Aristotle and Horace.

Moratín seems to be constantly surprised that everyone does not see the deplorable conditions of Spanish theater as clearly as he does. After all, these ideas are not new: "There have been written in Spain, England, France, and Italy such famous poetic treatises, that whoever looks at them objectively cannot help but condemn what is going on in our theaters. Of course someone will say that man is free to have his own opinions; and that if Aristotle voiced his opinion anyone else is free to contradict him. But this position is born of ignorance, because Aristotle did not invent his reasons nor did he create the rules. Rules were invented by nature itself, and Aristotle was only a mere observer of it . . . ."[4] He finished the remark by stating that "any idiot can do the same if he will stop to reflect upon it."

Moratín was heavily influenced by the ideas of Neoclassicism being discussed at the time. Luzán's ideas, of course, were still in vogue in the early 1760s, although they had been modified in the salons and academies of the capital, particularly in the Academy of Good Taste. Montiano and Velázquez were the most eloquent exponents of the new theories in drama and poetry in the preceding decade, and Moratín built on those ideas in his own theoretical works. In the first *Reproach* he provides no startlingly new ideas, but he does express his critical focus forcefully. Certain key words reappear — "perfection," "clarity," "imitation," "rules" — all of which are standard Neoclassical nouns. The purpose of theater is to deceive the spectator, but to do so with some semblance of verisimilitude. For Moratín, the trappings of theater — costumes, sets, gestures — come to nought when not supported by the author's attempts to avoid fakery in style, and here he moves the reader into his central preoccupation — the importance of rules.

"Who can believe what he is hearing; that, without moving, he has seen Madrid and Zaragoza? Who can be persuaded that he has seen things happen over many years...represented in live action?"[5] This is the core of what Moratín will repeat over and over again: theater and poetry need rules; rules are derived from nature; rules provide for decorous, reasonable art; literature without rules is frivolous, if not downright dangerous; it is imperative that rules be followed. Moratín's dependence on the rules and his belief in them is maintained until his death, even when he falls into absurdities while trying to defend or explain them; at one point he equates the rules of art with nature and then with God, presumably suggesting that it is anti-Christian to ignore those rules. This concept has enabled critics of Neoclassicism, both in the eighteenth century and today, to consider Neoclassic art not as "art for art's sake" or even "art for reason's sake," but as a type of "art for rules' sake." The accusation is valid up to a point, but it is invalid when used as an excuse to label an entire century's or individual's artistic production.

Moratín resorts to name-calling in order to make his points: whoever denies the simplicity of his statements on dramatic illusion is "an uncultured barbarian, inept, and blind to the light of reason."[6] He extends his polemical posture through examples, attacking such slips of good taste as when the *gracioso* interrupts tender or tragic scenes with his jokes. He is angered by those (unnamed) individuals who claim that the public will not tolerate "artistic" (here, of course, he means Neoclassical, or since the word was not yet used, written according to the rules) dramas; he is referring to Lope as well as to his own contemporary Ramón de la Cruz. To "prove" his point he quotes himself, stating that such arguments have been refuted in the prologue he wrote for his comedy *La petimetra,* which brings up what sounds like sour grapes: his play was never presented on stage because, according to him, those various *sainete*-makers and versifiers whom we've seen before "upon hearing that it is written according to the rules scorn it,"[7] and presumably influence the public, actors, and impresarios to turn away from it.

Yet it cannot be denied that he makes some excellent points and that he clearly states the growing concerns of Madrid's Neoclassical group. It was true that the art of acting was in a shambles and theater was, more and more, becoming spectacle, supported by singers, dancers, clowns, *entremeses,* and other nonserious diversions.[8] He vehemently disagrees with Lope's opinion, expressed in what Moratín cleverly calls "his absurd art of making comedies,"[9] that the populace is ignorant and needs to be entertained with an abundance of movement and activity on the stage. The people cannot be quite so ignorant, says Moratín, when they choose to pay money at the theater presenting the best dancers, not necessarily the best plays, thus emphasizing the lack of merit of the play (many times a Golden-Age play) being shown.

Moratín's major concern in this first *Reproach* is to bring attention to the serious decay in Spanish stage art by pointing out what he considered its major defects to be. Naturally, Lope receives criticism, primarily for his cavalier attitude toward the rules. From what information Moratín was receiving in his literary circles, educated individuals inside and outside Spain were laughing at the uncultured, barbaric productions of the great Golden-Age "masters." Italy and France especially had presented a clearer definition of dramatic art, and Moratín was sensitive to his country's being called ignorant. But his group had already received criticism in its attempts at correcting abuses by following examples from abroad ("those of us who write that way are called foreigners and deserters"[10]); here he is referring to Montiano's two attempts, *Virginia* and *Ataúlfo,* as well as to his own *La petimetra.*

Theater is not merely a matter of form. Although the violence done to the rules of art causes him great concern, he has higher goals: ". . . all these defects seem to be nothing when compared to a more serious one, which is the lack of moral instruction. After the pulpit, which is the chair of the Holy Spirit, there is no other school that can teach us more than the theater, but it is today wildly corrupt. It is the school of evil, the mirror of lasciviousness, the picture of lewdness, the academy of impudence, the exemplar of disobedience, insults, mischief, and deceit."[11] These oft-quoted lines sum up Moratín's anger at what the theater was, as opposed to what he thought it should be.

The thought that any father would let his daughter see these dramas, in which seducers, Don Juans, tricksters, and scoundrels were held up as heroes, was too much for him to bear: are these activities acceptable in "Catholic Theater"? And this is where Moratín reemphasizes his aesthetics and his religious politics, concepts not at all dissimilar in the mind of the Spanish Neoclassicists. "Catholic Theater." Of course there is no such thing, but Moratín — publicly, at least — would maintain a close, if not inseparable, relationship between art and morals. This was not a new argument. For years the religious community had railed against the evils of the stage and would do so for years to come, but it was the first time a fully secular segment of society had picked up this battle cry. No longer was moral instruction the sole concern of the Church; no longer would it be merely the clergy who protested moral turpitude; no longer would the institutions of Catholicism be the theater's only censors.

Moratín closes the first *Reproach* with a challenge: we can do it, he says, if we try. He wants his country to continue what certain individuals are starting (he and Montiano, again, although unnamed): to write plays, specifically tragedies, that are replete with invention, pleasure, and art (rules). "I would see come alive in my nation not only true Plautuses, Terences, Menandros, and Aristophanes, but Senecas, Euripides, Sophocles, and Aeschyluses"[12] — in short, a reflourishing of Classical, but, for the eighteenth century, Neo-Classical, drama.

So Moratín was seriously chastened by accusations, heard in his elite circles, that Spain was a nation of uncivilized barbarians which lacked any awareness of the fact that a new age in art was dawning. The intensely patriotic Moratín took the criticism to heart and what was in effect a campaign to "correct" the abuses of the Spanish theater (and if it had a positive effect on customs, so much the better) came to be interpreted as the railings of an enemy, of a type of negative Don Quijote gone berserk, whose goal was to destroy the reputation of Golden-Age playwrights.

He took Lope's *Arte nuevo de hacer comedias* (New Art of Playwriting) literally, ignoring the tongue-in-cheek nature of the piece, and subsequently launched a series of harsh criticisms of Lope and Calderón, whom he called the "principal corruptors"[13] of Spanish theater. Such explicit comments were startling enough to have been remembered out of context and eventually to have been used against him. Contemporary critics were no less harsh. The *Belianís Literario,* an anonymous journal, dedicated several pages to a critique of Moratín, whose *Reproach 1* was summed up in these terms: "But since it is not the same thing to think clearly and to write well, it is not strange that the scrupulous critic should find some faults [in Moratín's writing] like the lack of originality in his thoughts and reflections, the worn and commonplace nature of the proofs and authorities, and effeminacy and inconsistency of the style, reduced to a prolix and continuous narration, without method or separation of its various parts, without divisions, numbers, paragraphs, or chapters."[14]

In *Reproach 2* Moratín turns his attention more specifically to the one-act eucharistic plays of Calderón, the *autos sacramentales,* centering upon his own definition of art-by-the-rules. He begins the piece with some short definitions, or allusions to certain definitions that are "common knowledge": first of what dramatic poetry is, and second of which rules are the most important. In a series of rhetorical questions he provides a glimpse into his interpretation of dramatic poetry:

[Whoever would applaud the *autos*], does he know what poetry is and into what classes it is divided? Does he know what dramatic, or representable, poetry is? What its craft is? What parts make it up? What particulars it should have? What rules it should observe? What its purpose is? What means it should employ to achieve its goal? That authors here and abroad have dealt with this matter for centuries? Does he know those authors who have put them into practice more or less successfully? Has he collated the merit of their works and examined without prejudice the criticisms made of them? Does he know the beginnings and progresses of European theater, and of Latin and Greek theater? Does he know, at last, the philosophy of the human heart, its passions and movements, and the way to animate it with rhetorical artifice, and all the other qualities that a good dramatic poet should possess?[15]

Then his blow is dealt: "If he knows such things (and few people do, for the matter is not as easy as it seems), I am certain that he will not approve of the *autos.*"[16]

Rules are necessary and natural; this is the fundamental Neoclassical principle to which Moratín subscribes and which he repeats throughout his career. It is no doubt one he taught at the Imperial College; it is one he tried to follow in his own writings. Here, at the outset of his literary career, he is outspoken about the rules: "That [the *autos*] should observe some rules is dictated by natural reason"; "To say that the *autos,* and other theatrical pieces, need not be subjected to rules is a horrendous absurdity"; "I only search for one rule, the rule of rules, to which all the others are reduced, and that one rule is verisimilitude, or propriety; from which it may be inferred that the rules which reason and good taste have dictated should be observed, not because foreigners observe them, but because reason demands it."[17]

The groundwork prepared, Moratín then launches himself into a literal and lopsided analysis of the *autos,* pausing along the way to voice disagreement with some other Golden-Age productions. It is that verisimilitude, or theatrical illusion, that most troubles him. As he could not stand being shown characters moving from country to country, or aging precipitously, in popular drama, he reacts similarly to the *autos,* but more passionately, since their moral underpinnings are based on religious imagery. His *bête noire* becomes allegory. His oft-quoted lines read: "Is it possible for Spring to speak? Have you ever heard one word from Appetite? Do you know what the Rose's voice sounds like? Is the Cedar's voice gruff?"[18] Frankly, it was easy to be seduced by such literal reasoning, for the obvious answer to all the questions was "no." Moratín succeeded in confusing the issue and thereby rallying support. The problem with the *autos* was not a lack of rules but a lack of dignity in their presentation, a matter which he addressed later.

His flashy and somewhat hysterical comments attracted attention, strengthening his resolve to continue what had by now become a real campaign to have the presentation of the *autos* prohibited. Allegory, says he, is merely a pretext to cover up all manner of ridiculous and thoughtless ideas and absence of stagecraft; such being the case, Moratín wittily offers to write a drama and whenever he gets stuck, "I'll have the first pillar speak, or the guitarist's eyeglasses, or the prompter's underwear, or the usher's cape; and if they tell me that such a thing is folly I will respond that it is allegory...."[19] After all, he continues, it is the same to have shorts talking as it is to have justice, truth, reason, desire, Sunday, Monday, and Tuesday up on stage giving speeches. Obviously, Moratín is much more successful when using wit and humor than when employing insult and invective to prove his case, all of which he does with surprising frequency. He was not against Calderón's use of allegory; he was against the entire concept of allegory in dramatic productions (he accepts it in lyric and epic poetry). This is one place where he differs radically from Luzán, who wrote in 1737 in his *Poética:* "The *autos sacramentales* are another type of dramatic poetry known only in Spain; and its artifice reduces itself to forming an allegorical representation dealing with the sacrosanct mystery of the Eucharist, which, because it is pure allegory, is free from the major part of the rules of tragedy."[20]

For Moratín, violence done to the rules of drama is unacceptable in any form. Anachronism is uncalled for. Having divine beings speak on stage is outrageous. Jokesters carrying on in front of

Jesus is blasphemous. Saying that Christ died on Three Crosses Street in Madrid is heresy. Calderón is to be blamed for the most outrageous examples of dramatic laxity. It is unforgiveable to continue defending Calderón blindly: "Do not be ashamed to admit the truth, as I have, I who was in the same error; because an aunt of mine had me believing that there were no things greater than the *autos*; but I found out differently, and confessed the deceit: that Calderón was very Catholic and very learned, I do not deny; but that he gave us extremely poor examples in his plays I proved in my first *Reproach*."[21] Moratín's use of religious imagery underscores his position as more than a crusader for art. He mixes it freely with an underlying moral conception of Spanish society.

Yet he is so literal, which proves to be his undoing. He faults Calderón for anachronism or poor attributions of characteristics, yet he falls himself into the absurd statement, while commenting upon a speech by St. Paul in one of the *autos,* that "I know for certain that St. Paul was not so pedantic."[22] He reaches back to Calderón's *La vida es sueño* (Life Is a Dream) to support his point that Calderón knew nothing of verisimilitude, citing the fact that Rosaura, after careening down the precipice on her horse, does not complain of bumps and bruises but rather bursts forth with poetic images.

To those who would defend the *autos* as theology, Moratín responds that they would be much better off just reading the Bible, or, more interesting for our understanding of his critical positions, Racine's *Esther* and *Athalie,* where better ideas of religion are presented without the extravagances and monstrosities of the *autos.* This mention of Racine brings Moratín to a comparison between Calderón and another French dramatist, Corneille. The French Academy found Calderón a worthy peer of Corneille, but Moratín qualifies the comparison: Calderón certainly bested the Frenchman in imagination (without paying any attention to verisimilitude, of course), but in "Art" the Spaniard remains far below his northern counterpart. In fact, Moratín's *Reproach 2* seems to be written to the French as much as to his Spanish peers. He says, "Let foreigners know that Spaniards of judgement do not approve of such plays and that Don Pedro Calderón is not in charge of Spanish literature: there are others, both dead and alive, who overshadow him"[23]

It must be pointed out that Moratín is not blindly hostile to Lope and Calderón; it only seems that way since his criticisms tend to be rather dramatically stated. He does sprinkle his writings with praise for their achievements ("I do not deny that many praises of Calderón are justified"; "I do not deny that some delicate and very tender things can be found in the *autos*"), but always guardedly. Yet most important, as we shall see later, is the obvious integration of many of their very characteristics into his own works.

His arrogant attitude maintained,[24] he issues the call to arms that will become a mainstay of his artistic theory: let us do better; let us criticize but at the same time produce viable models; let us teach through example. He fears, however, that he is fighting a losing battle:

But in payment for my work you will see my ungrateful nation, fierce and cloaked, take up arms against me. Writers are already sharpening their pencils to annoy me with satires and taunts in their acrid diatribes. But what diatribes! You shall see! First they will call me French, then Italian, then English, and in such a way they will chase all over the map until they call me Chinese.[25]

Nevertheless, and although completely serious in his intention, he ends his second *Reproach* trenchantly: "If [my critics] judge this paper to be a fabric of mistakes with no order, or a string of audacities with no judgment, or a thicket of improprieties, nonsense, and deliriums, I will say what they say in order to defend the *autos*: I will say, simply, that it is allegory."[26] Moratín's intent to silence his critics merely brought the matter of the *autos* out into the open, and a vociferous polemic was initiated among various segments of Madrid's literary society. Clavijo and Moratín were the staunchest vilifiers of the *autos* while Cristóbal Romea y Tapia and Francisco Mariano Nipho came forth to defend them.

Romea's *El escritor sin título* (The Nameless Writer) was originally aimed at Clavijo's comments on Golden-Age theater, but Moratín's additions to the polemic[27] instigated Romea's response in his sixth installment, entitled *Desengaño al desengaño II* (Reproach to the Second Reproach). He had already taken shots at Moratín's "regular" plays, *La petimetra* and *Lucrecia,* in the second chapter of his work;[28] here he shows himself to be a believer in the dramatic legitimacy of the *autos,* and his defense is pointed and clever as he uses some of Moratín's own more outrageous statements against him. He attacks Moratín's definition of allegory, emphasizing particularly his supposed confusion of truth and verisimilitude, then provides nearly a line-by-line refutation of the "reproacher's" ideas. Moratín was not deterred.

Reproach 3, the longest of Moratín's attacks, presents a rein-
forcement of his previous positions: the theater is a mirror of customs and it is currently in a sorry state; rules of art are
indispensable; the *autos* are monstrosities, etc. Much of it is
tediously repetitive. It is replete with examples and appeals to the
authority of past authors (and, we note, they are *Spanish* authors):
Fray Luis de León, Herrera, Nebrija, and again, Montiano,
Nasarre, and Luzán. The unscholarly beginning ("Didn't I tell you
this would happen? Well, it turned out just as I predicted"[29]) leads
into what he supposes is a refutation of Romea's comments. He
does, however, Hispanize his commentary in this *Reproach,* sensitive once again to the accusations thrown at him that he was some
sort of foreigner: "...in order to know the most delicate aspects of
Art, it is not necessary to turn to Boileau or to Fontenelle, because
here we have original artists."[30]

As to Romea's truth/verisimilitude idea, Moratín states: "I have
already said that I seek no rules other than verisimilitude or
propriety, because in my opinion, without getting into pedantries,
anything that is verisimilar, appropriate, natural or believable is
good for the theater...."[31] He is best, here as in the second
Reproach, when he satirizes the *autos* by offering to write two himself, and letting them be judged accordingly. One will follow
closely the established custom; hence, it will contain puerile allusions, anagrams, profanations, anachronisms, oddities, and the
like. It will take place everywhere, from East to West; it will
develop, in three short hours, everything which has gone on since
Genesis to the Final Judgment; it will cover nothing less than Universal history. The other *auto* will be reasonable, subjected to the
rules, and infinitely better. But who shall judge them? Ah, impossible task in today's world: barbarous, uncultured and ignorant
people shall have no vote. Leave it up to the academies of Madrid,
Paris, London, and Rome. The whole issue was a hollow dare, of
course, but it did neatly synthesize his views on what to do and
what not to do, as well as who is and who is not capable of judging
acceptable drama.[32]

While Moratín claimed to be just another author and theater critic, his attacks on the *autos* once again carried theological overtones. That is, he did not object merely to their form, but also, as
he saw it, to the blasphemous interpretations of Catholic dogma
and of Christian faith. He felt that the allegory and the patently

anachronistic representations violated religious sentiment and therefore nullified the *autos* as effective, or even acceptable, theater.[33]

Many of the ideas presented in the three *Reproaches* were not original. Much of what Moratín wrote about the *autos* was paraphrased from what Clavijo had written earlier (Clavijo was the first to call Lope and Calderón "corruptors of the theater," for example). Moratín's belief that the Spaniards were laughed at abroad most likely came directly from Clavijo, who, unlike Moratín, had lived in France for years. Nasarre, whom Moratín cites three times, had previously called the *autos* "monstrosities" (in the 1749 prologue to his edition of Cervantes's plays). Montiano had called for (and written) Neoclassical tragedies. López Sedano's prologue to his 1763 play, *Jahel,* voiced condemnations of the "monstrosities" that abounded in the *comedia.* What Moratín did was to recombine ideas that had been getting some attention in literary circles and make them public, adding to them his own examples, his unshakable conviction on the rightness of his position, and his wit. Why was this all happening precisely in the early 1760s? The Neoclassicists had not yet achieved any degree of celebrity or of power, but they had become by then a cohesive and identifiable group. The subject was "in the air," so to speak, and the matter of the *autos* was fed no doubt by a multiple-volume reprinting of them initiated in 1760.[34]

The authorities Moratín cites in his dissertations are varied, but heavily dependent on both Spanish and ancient Greek and Roman sources: 38 percent of those he uses to support his contentions are Spanish sixteenth-century humanists and poets (Pinciano, Fray Luis, Nebrija, Herrera, Jáurequi, Broncense); 6 percent are contemporary Neoclassicists (Nasarre, Luzán, Mayans, Montiano); 38 percent are Greeks and Romans (Anacreon, Ovid, Aristotle, Homer, Terence, Plautus); 9 percent are French (Racine, Corneille, Boileau); 8 percent are Italians (Ariosto, Boyard, Metastasio); and the rest an assortment of saints, Classical figures, and painters. Moratín was obviously aware of what was transpiring abroad, but his most direct sources were traditional Classical authors and his own country's Renaissance and contemporary writers (fully 44 percent of the total).

The *Reproaches* were undeniably controversial and they have been remembered as important, angry, muddleheaded or effective, depending upon who is doing the remembering. From the British perspective, recorded after the appearance of Nicolás's *Post-humous Works* in 1825, the *Reproaches* "drove away all prejudices, and established greater freedom and greater latitude for the efforts of those individuals who succeeded them in the dramatic horizon."[35] Menéndez Pelayo is likewise charitable in his commentary on them, and Castrovido expressed some chagrin that Moratín has "never been forgiven" and therein lies the "principal cause of the harshness of criticism"[36] leveled at him. In some quarters today he has not fared so well: Entrambasaguas states:

And so it can be seen that in the eighteenth century masonry, represented, without a doubt, by Clavijo Fajardo — who used as the visible head the empty and vain one of the mediocre writer don Nicolás Fernández de Moratín, whose only lasting work was his son Leandro — the supression of the *autos sacramentales* was achieved. . . .[37]

Moratín's defense of regulated theater and attacks on the *autos* were never based on any organized philosophical trends, masonry included. That Moratín would be accused of "masonic" thought is as unacceptable as his being considered a handmaiden of Voltaire, particularly in light of how Voltaire was interpreted in eighteenth-century Spain. Heterodoxy and impiety were not aspects of Moratín's character, as he clearly reveals by mixing his social criticism with his defense of religious custom.

Alborg correctly points out that the general campaign against the *autos* was based on two concepts, one literary and one moral.[38] They were both fundamental concerns of the Neoclassicists, and, although different, they were tightly related in Moratín's mind: correct form was a result of, and led to, reasonable thinking, which likewise resulted from, and produced, judicious behavior. Hence a chain was forged, with the theater being a major link. Moratín's ideas on the theater often closely paralleled Carlos III's enlightened and despotic ideas on politics — that theater should be for the people, but without them. That is, the active role was to be taken by authors, actors, and critics; the people were to be passive recipients of the lessons conveyed.[39] This was the old and oft-repeated idea of theater as a mirror to society, so any reform of society presupposed a reform of the theater; at least it was a supposedly easier task to undertake. They were, after all, literary people, not politicians.

II   *Prologues and Discourses*

It is difficult to separate Moratín's *Reproaches* from his other theoretical writings since they differ only mildly in tone, and not at all in substance. The most significant of these publications is the prologue that precedes his 1762 comedy *La petimetra,* for it is here that Moratín first states the reformist focus of his theatrical goals. In a preliminary letter written to the Duchess of Medinasidonia, Moratín states: "I was determined to purge the *comedia* of all improprieties,"[40] leaving little doubt as to the reason he undertook the task of playwriting. He models his play after (and the order is his) "the most Classical authors, Greeks, Latins, Italians and French, who have earned applause all over Europe."[41] He was fully conscious of the newness and of the difficulty of his undertaking. That it might not be well received he clearly understood ("I only need some powerful protection to defend me against the public's obstinacy"[42]), but no matter — he had his goals in mind and he meant to reach them.

The dissertation itself contains many of the ideas that would receive wider attention when he repeated them in the *Reproaches* — that foreigners made fun of Spanish drama, that rules of art were essential, that Lope and Calderón knew those rules but chose to ignore them, that instruction was one of the key ends of art, and so on. The prologue betrays the arrogance of youth. Moratín is sure of himself, clear-spoken, and definite in his ideas. This was a rather audacious undertaking for a twenty-five-year-old, who was new to the capital (he had been there only two years).

Why did he expose himself to attack with this daring and polemical writing? Love of country, he claims, and the desire to vindicate Spanish drama, which, notwithstanding the talents of Lope, Calderón, Moreto, Solís, Candamo, "and others," lacks a single "perfect" play. He is much less harsh with the Golden-Age masters here than he will be in future treatises, stating his admiration for them and recognizing their genius. In fact, he waxes positively rapturous in praise of them, particularly over their non-dramatic productions:

Who could not like and be charmed by that prodigious fluency, so natural, and abundant of the profound Calderón, by whose sweet voice the muses spoke delicacies? Who does not admire the discretion of Solís, of don Francisco de Roxas, of don Agustín Moreto, of Candamo, of Montalvan, and many others? And who would be idiot enough not to admire amazed the natural facility and the sonorous elegance of the very fecund Lope, who was so excellent in lyric verse that he cedes no advantages to Petrarch? In heroic verse he was sublime. . . . I have no hate or envy for these esteemed men. . . . [43]

Moratín's dramatic theories changed very little over the course of his short life, and the prologue to *La petimetra* clearly states the major points of his critical concerns. There existed certain artistic absolutes, primarily in the "natural" precepts of drama and poetry, yet no one had ever systematically applied them to the writing of original comedies in Spain. On the contrary Lope claimed to have systematically avoided them, a thought that angered and shamed Moratín, and which he sought to prove misguided.

The excuse that [Lope] gives does not seem to me worthy of his great intelligence, since he says he wrote "without art" to please the public and to entertain the ignorant masses; but I cannot believe that although the masses may enjoy something unregulated (and I do not deny that this does happen) they would not enjoy something else only because it is constructed artfully. . . . There is no reason why the people should dislike a comedy or tragedy merely because it maintains the three unities of time, place, and action. [44]

He cites Molière, Metastasio, Goldoni, and his own mentor, Montiano, to support his thesis, although he seems to believe that the latter's *Virginia* and *Ataúlfo* were more popular than they actually were. "To please the public it is not necessary to abandon Art." [45]

Montiano was one of Moratín's influential masters. His clearest expression of his respect for Montiano appears in the 1765 poem *Diana.* His mentor may have died during the writing of the poem, for near the end of it (Canto VI, strophes 378-85), in a section which has nothing to do with the hunt, Moratín suddenly explodes into an unexpected elegy for "my sweet departed friend." In a series of personal inquiries and exclamations Moratín recalls their close association: Do you remember when we spoke together? Was it you with whom I consulted on my works and yours? What things I would ask you from our past conversations, etc. He credits Montiano with establishing the honor of Spanish theater again and admits that he (Moratín) learned from him and followed him, yet he also recognizes that Montiano's experiment failed to capture the respect of his country: "...But you could not conquer / The ungrateful people of our callous country." This lament applies equally to Moratín, although he would not fully realize it until twelve years later, in 1777, the year of his tragedy *Guzmán the Brave.* The Montiano section of *Diana* is, if misplaced, nonetheless moving and sincere, and it provides a brief firsthand look into their respectful and mutually influential relationship.

Rules for their own sake are one thing, Moratín continues in the prologue to *La petimetra,* and any impropriety produced due to lack of artistic exactness is fair game for critical attack. So are the conduct and acting skills of the actors themselves, but that is quite another matter. Playwriting and acting are not the same skills and Neoclassicists tended to confuse the two, or rather to confuse the issue by firing salvos against *what* was to be acted and *how* it was to be acted in the same work, often even in the same sentence.

The literal nature of Moratín's artistic views is clear in this essay, particularly in his demand for faithful maintenance of the Classical unities. He attempts to convince his readers that people are disturbed by theatrical irregularities such as seeing a child become a man in three hours, or being asked to believe that a suit of clothes lasts thirty or forty years. He is fully aware that his observations are not new, and that since Aristotle and all his intellectual disciples, including Cervantes, Cascales, Luzán ("who is more esteemed by foreigners than by Spaniards"), Mayans, Montiano, and a host of others, intelligent men have been commenting on the need for artistic precepts. But his answer is that it has been, apparently, all in vain since comedies still appear which ignore all that which has been written. Moratín's most immediate precursors are Montiano (who wrote a "severe, although extremely fair critique of Spanish authors"[46]) and Luzán, whose *Poetica* Moratín knew well. Leandro was wrong to suggest that Luzán was forgotten; at least he was not by Nicolás: "The celebrated Luzán wrote a separate chapter on the most common defects of our *comedias;* and although in some ways it will seem that I am repeating what this great poet said, I will mention some of them briefly...."[47]

Moratín's solutions to the supposed problems of the unities will become evident as we study his plays, but he gives hints as to how he will handle certain matters. A dream sequence in which several men are seen and heard in widely disparate places could be better handled as a narrated tale, he writes. He attacks the lack of verisimilitude in those frequent scenes in which the hero speaks at length with a masked lady, not recognizing her to be his very own sister, or fiancée, or whatever. Yet we shall soon see that Moratín, while avoiding this particular inverisimilitude, fell into others in the very play which this commentary precedes. Theory is easier than practice, and notwithstanding his continuous repetition of this truth as a challenge to his critics, it took him years to figure it out for himself.

"The purpose of poetry is to instruct pleasantly, and the same goes for the *comedia*."[48] This was a keystone idea for the Neoclassicists, picked up from Spanish Classical and ancient authorities. Didacticism and moral instruction were among the hallmarks of the European Enlightenment, and even more so in Spain, where the influence of the Church and the need for a stable, moral monarchy was seldom questioned. Lope and Calderón certainly knew the rules of art, especially those directed toward correcting vices, but they capriciously ignored them. This is where Moratín becomes most severe with his predecessors, here and in the *Reproaches;* he is outraged and somewhat puzzled that these illustrious playwrights should have willfully refused to write their dramas in accordance with the rules that were, at least for Moratín, essential, obvious, natural, and reasonable. His blind spot was that of the Neoclassicist: he could not see (perhaps just not accept) why anyone would *not* adhere to those eminently sensible rules.

So his drama *La petimetra* would follow the rules ("written with all the precision of art," as the title page declares), be morally instructive, and animate others to follow his example. Ironically, while he attacks Lope for pandering to the will of the people, he recognizes that his drama, too, will include some concessions to popular taste: "I have separated myself from common dramas where all the characters are lovers, duelers, and prettyboys; but I have not forgotten them completely, since they suit the nation's taste and character."[49]

Similar precepts are discussed in the prologue to his next play, a tragedy entitled *Lucrecia.* Just a year had passed since the publication of *La petimetra,* but since Moratín could not get his comedy staged he gamely turned to tragedy, hoping to have better luck. As he had done in the prologue to the comedy, and would soon do in the *Reproaches,* he appeals to the authority of ancient Classical and Spanish authors to support his contentions. Here Ovid is initially cited to underscore the dignity of the tragic genre, and to feign surprise that tragedies are not held in as high esteem at home as they are in Italy, France, England, and even Germany. As conscious as he was of Greek, Latin, and Spanish models, he also left room for appeal to French precedent by citing Corneille, Racine, and even, not really surprisingly, demonstrating a knowledge of Voltaire.

In this prologue Moratín reveals the wit and sarcasm, almost Olympian and certainly patronizing at times, which would be glaringly evidenced in the *Reproaches*. "I well know that in Spain it is commonly believed that poetry is not a science, nor should it be studied, and that any witty and joking scoundrel who finds a consonant is taken for a Virgil, being, at best, a mere poetaster or versifier, which is far from being a poet...."[50] Yet withal, Moratín sounds almost defeatist in this prologue, sure that he will not produce a quality tragedy (after all, a perfect tragedy is "one of the most noble productions of human nature"[51]), and only hoping to incite others to do better. He seems to have been chastened by the indifferent or possibly hostile reaction to *La petimetra* since he repeats the canard that criticism is easy, art is difficult — and besides, he writes, he does not presume to be successful at everything.

Nevertheless undaunted, he continues his reasoning, justifying the need for this tragedy written in accordance with all sensible ancient and modern precepts, which civilized nations have adopted. His intention is to show through example, not merely by loudly criticizing what was done. This goal apparently failed, since the *Reproaches* are mostly criticism and very little example; he certainly never undertook the writing of an "acceptable" *auto sacramental*. But it is impossible to fault his intentions when he claims: "It seemed to me that our *comedias* were utterly ruined by the abandonment of the rules of theater; and so I did not content myself with pointing them out, but rather, as I could, I put them into practice. Now I am doing the same with tragedies. I would ask whoever dislikes mine to do another, which might serve as a model that I might imitate...."[52] He congratulates himself for keeping to the rules and maintaining the three unities.

It is here that Moratín talks about "taste," although the words "good taste" appeared on the first page of *La petimetra* (Damián discusses Jerónima's "good taste" in her manner of dress). As we have seen, it was never fully developed as a Neoclassical concept. It is the background against which Moratín's thoughts are reflected, and that which outlines many of the other Neoclassicists' critical postures, most obviously those who grouped themselves into the

Academy of Good Taste. Good taste was an elusive concept and ill-defined, but it contained certain elements that have come to be closely related to Neoclassical aesthetics. Rules, decorum, natural-ness, verisimilitude, rationality, clarity of expression, even a touch of literary elitism were the central elements of Moratín's conception of literary creation, coupled with study of the appropriate models and "art." In short, it was, for them, merely the exercise of common sense. No one ever bothered to define it. It was simply one of those characteristics which, apparently, those who had knew they had and which they so actively sought to encourage others to get. Leandro includes it among such noble qualities as utility, healthy criticism, and erudition.[53] It was something that could be acquired, through serious study and, presumably, a little help from the Neoclassicists. Nicolás's poetry lessons at San Isidro were geared toward its acquisition. The *Gaceta de Madrid* (December 24, 1771) even announced a calligraphy course directed at forming letters with "good taste." It pervaded intellectual undertakings in the 1760s and 1770s, but it was not, as B. Jarnés would have us think, a "passion for the foreign."[54] Joaquín Arce most perceptively defines good taste as an aesthetic and an ethical ideal[55] in which a sort of balance is achieved between the artfulness of the literary creation and its concurrence with Enlightened thought. And Moratín's own theoretical writings become a definition-in-reverse by attacking all which was "bad taste" — extravagance, pedantry, superficiality, absence of rules, mixture of genres, bad timing, inverisimilitude, and so on. Whether he himself escapes the pitfalls of bad taste we shall soon see.

The prose prologues to his poetry collection, the *Poet* (1764) and to *Diana* (1765) reveal similar concerns, although they are more self-justification than critical inquiry. His main critique is directed again at the "prodigious multitude of works by those versifiers and poetasters who have inundated Spain in the past century and the present one."[56] That critical stance appeared clearly in several of the poems from the former work, particularly the oft-cited three satires which appeared in the third, sixth, and ninth installments of the periodical. In the tercets of the first satire the satirical Castilian muse ("not ugly / If her influence is directed toward a noble end"[57]) appears to Moratín in a dream. She counsels him to take up arms (his pen) against the corruptors of society, since verse can lead toward society's perfection, in somewhat the same manner that theater can present good models and correct many vices.

Vuelve los ojos, vuelve al patrio muro,
Verásle en mil errores sumergido,
De los cuales sacarle yo procuro.
¿No adviertes entre el tráfago y ruido,
Que la hispana metrópoli alborota,
El noble y el plebeyo confundido?
¿No ves que la verdad está remota,
Porque de tus patricios la enajena
La envidia que veneno infernal brota?
¿No adviertes cómo audaz se desenfrena
La juventud de España corrompida
De Calderón por la fecunda vena?
¿No ves a la virtud siempre oprimida
Por su musa en el cómico teatro,
Y la maldad premiada y aplaudida...? (BAE, 31)

(Turn your eyes, turn to your country,
And see it submerged in a thousand errors,
From which I shall try to save it.
Don't you perceive among the traffic and noise,
That the Hispanic metropolis clamors,
The nobleman and peon are confused?
Don't you see that truth is remote,
Because envy, gushing infernal poison, whisks it
Away from your compatriots?
Don't you perceive how daringly Spanish
Youth becomes ungoverned, corrupted by the
Prolific vein of Calderón?
Don't you see Virtue always suppressed
By the comic theater's muse and
Evil rewarded and applauded....?)

He goes on to decry what he had so shrilly stated in the *Reproaches* — Spain was ridiculed for her stupid plays, the theater was corrupt, art and rules were ignored, and fantasy reigned. He continues to attack current customs, particularly the Frenchified *petimetra,* that silly lady whom he satirized in his first play. He was horrified that Spanish youth apparently took certain cues from the Golden-Age dramas they were used to seeing, acting publicly the part of the frivolous lovers, the valient and dashing swordsmen, the secretive citizens. It should not be difficult for us to understand the concerns of these would-be reformers, since our own society hears continuous outcries against drugs, sex, and violence in film, television, or printed matter.

All this apparently led to Moratín's statement in Satire 2 (for Menéndez Pelayo an awful poem, for Cotarelo one of Moratín's best) that "everything is...haughtiness and impertinence. / ... / More evil reigns in this century, if that's possible, / Than in Rome's most lascivious times..." (BAE, 32), a disturbingly negative and frustrated view of Spanish society. Moratín was a Cassandra, seeing corruption everywhere encouraged by bad poetry and drama and viewing the reform of society from a literary perspective. "They applaud the licentious *comedia* / That extends itself to approving vice / And makes bold life acceptable." And what happens to the author who attempts to write a moral comedy (read this as his response to the reception of *La petimetra*)?

> Mas la que enlaza el cómico artificio,
> Y aplaude las virtudes, reprendiendo
> Los yerros, que nos sirven de perjuicio;
> En que castiga al áspero y horrendo
> Traidor, o al alevoso fementido
> Con suplicio crüel su error tremendo;
> O vitupera al falso y atrevido
> Amante engañador, y premia en ella
> Al virtüoso, al cuerdo y comedido;
> No solo no se admite, se atropella,
> Se desprecia, se infama, y aun acaso
> Contra el autor se forma una querella. (BAE, 32)

> (But the comedy that upholds comic artifice,
> And applauds virtue, reprimanding
> Errors, that serve our prejudices;
> In which the harsh and horrible traitor,
> Or the unfaithful scoundrel is punished
> With cruel torment for his horrible ways;
> Or the false and daring seducer is
> villified, and the virtuous, sensible
> And gentle man is rewarded;
> Not only are these plays not accepted, they
> Are insulted, despised, defamed, and even perhaps
> There begins a quarrel against the author.)

He concedes that things theatrical are not as violent as they were in pagan days, but he minces no words when railing against the "insufferable evils, continuous thievery and horrifying actions" current on the stage of his day. What horrible lessons these plays teach: "That is where licentiousness, vanity / And scandalous arrogance is learned'' (33). He severely criticizes Lope again: ''Do not name Terence and Plautus, / There is an ignoramus here who despises them, / Because their style is clear: don't be shocked.''

If the first two satires repeat what he had written elsewhere, the third openly enjoins the battle over the theater which was still raging. His opening verse agressively paraphrases Quevedo:[58] ''I will not keep quiet, even though you threaten me'' (33). The tone here is polemical, angry, and clear, with allusions to *La pensadora gaditana* (The Thinker from Cadiz) and *The Nameless Writer*. He appears to be fed up with the adulation of idiots and the lack of attention and respect accorded true thinkers and artists (presumably he counts himself among the latter) by certain self-appointed critics. The failure of his own two dramas brings forth this wry observation: ''I would be very loved by everyone / If only I had stuck to criticism, / And no one had seen my dramas.'' And wry it is, since nobody did see his dramas on the stage, although they were circulated in print and sufficiently well known to be criticized: ''And instead of looking at what I try / To say when I reproach the theater / You conjure up my own scenes. / And finding a defect (not surprising / Since I never denied being fallible, / Exposed to ignorance and to deceit). / With shouts and terrible jubilation / You show your friends and servants / The errors of the inflexible critic'' (34). So he will not keep quiet, and does not.

Moratín's activities in the first half of the 1760s centered upon his fervent desire to follow the lead of Nasarre, Montiano, and others in substituting useful, moral theater for the vice-ridden plays which they saw dominating the Spanish stage. From 1762 to 1766 he produced a stream of critical discourses attached to or integrated into some original plays and poems, plus three important treatises on dramaturgy and the *autos sacramentales*. In these he was at times lucid and well stated, at times sarcastic and patronizing, at times furiously critical. And always he was literal, particularly when dealing with the allegory of the *autos* or the need for rules.

The campaigns against the *autos* were successful, in a short-term way, in that their performances were abolished by royal decree in June 1765.[59] It was a major victory for the Neoclassicists, who were on their way toward their goal of total defeat of the opposing literary camps, headed, they thought, by Ramón de la Cruz. Soon Aranda would establish the Royal Sites for Neoclassical dramas and give his protection to the Madrid authors seeking to have their original dramas staged, Moratín among them. What had been the

Neoclassical doctrines as articulated by Clavijo and Moratín came to be the guiding principles of theatrical activity in the late 1760s. Before he was thirty years old, Nicolás Fernández de Moratín became an extremely influential voice in the direction that Spanish literature was to take for the next four decades.

CHAPTER 3

Flumisbo, Poet

MORATÍN'S achievements in lyric and narrative poetry are significant. His sensitivity to the echoes of Classical verse, combined with his interest in reestablishing its wide acceptance and in updating its content, led him to the rediscovery of verse forms not in general use. He was seduced by the beauty of the anacreontic ode, a form that he handled with pleasant results; his have been judged "among the century's best,"[1] although the trumpet calls of epic verse likewise laid claim to his attentions. He wrote sonnets, epigrams, elegies, ballads, *silvas,* eclogues, satires, *décimas,* and *quintillas.* He was attracted to conventional themes — death, war, love, honor — but onto those he grafted an innate love for the Spanish national sport — the bullfight — and the very real passions he felt for his Dorisa.

Who was Dorisa? For some, the name anagrammatically hides that of his wife Isidora. Cotarelo put forth the case that it was Francisca Ladvenant, whose real first name was also Isidora. The evidence in Moratín's poetry suggests the latter to be the case, since Dorisa's youth, bright voice, and frequent absences are continuously commented upon by the poet. There is no evidence that Isidora was able to sing, and since she was only one year younger than her husband, her youth should presumably not be an issue; Francisca, on the other hand, was more than a dozen years his junior. Even more important is the fact that Moratín was not a faithful husband and, although there is no reason to believe that his relationship with his wife was not a workable one, nowhere in his writings does he write of her or of the joys of conjugal love. If his wife were the Dorisa who inspired him to such lofty heights of emotion and sentiment, we would expect those feelings to be intermingled with comments on the peace, excitement, pleasures, or advantages of the institution of marriage. In actual fact, his comments on marriage are frequently harsh and cynical, revealing his

71

belief that it was a despotic institution. As Cotarelo comments, this would have been a "strange way" of celebrating his wife. Leandro, while talking about Cadalso's Filis, fails even to mention his father's Dorisa, a surprising silence indeed if the lady were his mother.

Dorisa, more than anyone else, motivated Moratín's early poetic endeavors. Her eyes, her graceful demeanor, her seductive voice, and her youth all conspired to enchant him and to evoke from him soft musings of romantic love. Moratín met her shortly after his arrival in Madrid in 1759.[2] Sister of the "divine" María, she was a singing actress with the Madrid company of Nicolás de la Calle, and barely thirteen years old when Moratín wrote his first two plays. The "Eclogue to Velasco and González" of 1763 contains a reference to her and from then on he wrote a continuous stream of verses cautiously documenting their love affair. She appeared in the *Poet* frequently, the *Diana* of 1765, and the *Whores' Art* of 1771-72. Although married herself, she remained "faithful" to Moratín, staying as close to Madrid as her profession would permit and involving herself in his life. She was a member of Juan Ponce's company when it performed *Hormesinda* in 1770, but she was taken ill shortly thereafter and forced to retire to the hot springs in Valencia. There she died on April 11, 1772, at the early age of twenty-two. The date is almost exactly one year after the tragic loss of her friend María Ignacia Ibáñez (Filis), the mourned lover of Moratín's friend José Cadalso.[3] These four — Moratín, Cadalso, Dorisa, and Filis — enjoyed a close friendship for the brief time they were together in Madrid, a friendship particularly important in 1770, when Cadalso fell in love with his Filis. Like her, Dorisa was a real person, not another of the many Silvias or Amarillises so superficially popular with pastoral poets. Both women constantly reappear in the poetry of Cadalso and Moratín, at times even together: Cadalso sings of them in two anacreontic odes to Moratín (BAE, 61, pp. 272, 274), and Moratín responds with these delicate verses written to honor Cadalso's Saint's Day (March 19, 1771):

> Hoy celebro los días
> De mi dulce poeta,
> Del trágico Dalmiro
> Blasón de neustra escena.
> Venga la hermosa Filis
> Y mi Dorisa venga;
> Dorisa la que canta
> Con la voz de sirena. (BAE, 7)

(Today I shall honor
My sweet poet's day,
My tragic Dalmiro
The glory of our stage.
Come the lovely Filis,
And my Dorisa rejoice;
Dorisa, the one who sings
With the siren's voice.)

Over and over again Moratín writes of Dorisa. Her eyes and her voice wrenched from him his clearest visual images. Her eyes were "beautiful," "sparkly," "divine fires," "clear," "vibrant," "loving," and so on. Not for a moment do we believe his disclaimer, in a sonnet entitled "Platonic Love" (*PW*, 98; BAE, 17), that it was not her "rich" hair, her "virginal" cheeks, her "amber" lips, her "pearly" teeth, or her "divine lights" which seduce him, but rather her virtue and her sovereign soul. But their relationship had to remain relatively covert, or at least discreet. Both of them, after all, were married to other people and it would have been unseemly for them to carry on in public. Yet the affair was hardly private since Moratín broadcast his feelings for Dorisa in his printed verses, and even evoked her counsel in his scandalous manuscript poem, *The Whores' Art*. Nevertheless, it appears that Moratín's own conjugal situation was, by 1770, merely one of convenience, and he apparently felt free to pursue his interests outside the marriage bed. Only two poems in the *Poet* deal with matrimony; one is a translation of a sonnet by Goldoni *(Poet,* 5; BAE, 17), and the other is a dull *silva* on the marriage of María Luisa de Borbón *(Poet,* 8; BAE, 19–20). That he was an avid womanizer will become evident when we study the *Whores' Art,* and this vice was, it has now become apparent, transmitted to his son Leandro.[4]

Apart from the "Eclogue to Velasco and González" of 1763, the *Diana* of 1765, four poems honoring Garcilaso which Conti published in 1771, the three poems written for the awards ceremonies of the Royal Economic Society in 1777, 1778, and 1779, and a couple of occasional verses, the poems in *The Madrilenian Poet* were the only ones published during Moratín's lifetime. After his death, "Cortés's Ships" appeared, under the auspices of the Royal Printing Press, and much later more poems were gathered by Leandro for the *Posthumous Works* of 1821 and 1825, although Leandro did not include in his edition many of those poems already available in the *Poet.* Manuel José Quintana reprinted eight of what he considered to be Moratín's best in the third edition of his *Poesías selectas castellanas* (Selected Spanish Poems), volume 4 (Madrid, 1830), and Buenaventura Carlos Aribau reedited all he could find for his BAE volume. Aribau combined the *Poet,* the *PW,* the Quintana tome, and the separately published pieces into what has become the standard collection of Moratín's works.[5] René Foulché-Delbosc discovered five of Moratín's poems among Cadalso's papers and published them in 1892, and a very few poems have remained unpublished, tucked away in the far reaches of the Biblioteca Nacional in Madrid. None of the publishers, of course, printed (or even mentioned) the joco-serious *The Whores' Art,* which was finally published for the first time in 1898.

I El Poeta Matritense: *Dorisa in Installments*

The Madrilenian Poet represents a broad selection of Moratín's early concerns. Published from 1764 to 1766 in ten short installments, this poetry periodical offers a wide range of themes and meters, and an arrangement significantly different from that offered either by Leandro in 1821 or by Aribau in the BAE. In the *Poet* the order is in diversity as Moratín attempts to provide his readers with an enjoyable selection of *silvas,* sonnets, anacreontic odes, ballads, and other verse forms. He succeeds: the poems are thoughtful, seductive, polemical, or humorous, according to his mood. He is engaging and evasive, tackling once again the sins of the contemporary theater or luxuriating in the wonders of love. The *Poet* contains only fifty-three poems, but they represent nearly 50 percent of Moratín's total poetry production, excepting those works published separately. Of the thirty-nine anacreontic odes he wrote, nineteen are here; so, too, are five of his ten epigrams, thirteen of his twenty-six sonnets, both heroic ballads, two of the six *silvas,* two of the three elegies, four of the ten odes, all four satires, and his only *décima.* The collection established him as the leading poet in Madrid's young literary generation.

In the prologue he justifies his new endeavor, citing the need in Spain for "excellent" poetry based on "invention, artifice, study, imitation," and "purity of language," and the very first poem in the series is a kind of *ars poetica* in which he outlines his intention to cover a gamut of topics *(Poet,* 1; BAE, 19).[6] His verses will include love ("my amorous passion"), festivities, shepherds, truths, popular matters, patriotic themes, and epic themes. We shall see that for the most part he remains faithful to his stated goals. He will later pass through a stage in which he disdains epic themes (*Poet,* 3, BAE, 1; *Poet,* 4, BAE, 14; *Poet,* 7, BAE, 3), but he triumphantly returns to them for his "Cortés's Ships Destroyed." This first *silva* is conceptually interesting for it is a microcosmic Moratín: he sees himself as a poet; he banters with his readers; he leans heavily on Classical poetic tradition by using a remembrance of Virgil as a focal point; he unequivocally states his interest in Spanish affairs ("And my numerous verses shall praise / The country, and her most famous sons," 19); and he is somewhat disingenuous.

The overblown flattery of the reader rings false in a man who had previously considered himself to be an arbiter of what popular taste should be when he refused to capitulate to the public taste. He always chose to lead the taste of the common man, not follow it. He is more conciliatory here then he was when he wrote the prologues to *La petimetra* and *Lucrecia,* or in the *Reproaches,* where his attitude was one of refusing to suffer fools. Here, his reader's nobility "equals the king's"; but of course anyone reading his poetry has, *ipso facto,* good taste. He says that the dedication which he is writing will stray from the tradition of the "cultured pompous dedications" of pedantic authors — his will be aimed at the wise judgments of his audience. He will please his audience. Is he aware that he is slipping dangerously close to a position which he has already criticized severely, that of Lope's *Arte nuevo?* This give-them-what-they-want attitude is hardly what we expect to discover in Flumisbo. Yet that is precisely the source of the poetry's success. He is never unmindful of three important tenets: please the public, follow the models, and strive for "good taste." His dramas ignored the first tenet and suffered as a consequence.

One of the *Poet's* dominant themes is writing itself. The initial *silva* lays out what he will write about, and he follows up that idea in several anacreontic odes (BAE numbers 1, 2, 3, 16, 28, 29, 30, 35, 39), a pair of sonnets (23, 24), and all four satires. One major change is that he becomes less entranced with themes of war, once love has entered his poetic universe.

> Yo a cantar me aprestaba
> Las armas españolas,
> De Cortés y Pizarro
> Las ínclitas victorias.

A nuestro ardor sujetos
Los reinos de la aurora,
Las gentes dominadas,
Las tributarias flotas. *(Poet,* 3; BAE, 1)

(I used to be inclined to sing
 Of Spanish weaponry
 Of Cortés and of Pizarro
 Their distinguished victories.
 And to our courage subjected
 The kingdoms of the East,
 The dominated peoples,
 The tributary fleets.)

His muse informs him that he will end up writing about his "amorous passion" instead. But she adds another element which reveals Moratín to be a true child of the enlightened eighteenth century: she suggests that to achieve fame as a poet and to be worthy of the name he must "clean up Madrid of vice," of sloth, of "extravagant behavior." In part that will become his goal as it was in the *Reproaches* and in *La petimetra.* All of the satires *(Poet,* 2, 3, 6, 9; BAE, 31-5) deal with the goal of cleaning up the capital, centering themselves upon the immorality of the Spanish stage, the incompetence of Spanish playwrights, and the ineptitude of loud-mouthed critics.

Critics, as we saw in his prose treatises, command his attention in a noticeably hostile manner. Criticism is easy, he repeats, while good writing is difficult; consequently there is a paucity of both good writing and good criticism *(Poet,* 2; BAE, 1). Poetry is poorly received ("You will now rest in the hands / Of those who criticize / Who without reading all the works / At once push them aside" *Poet,* 7; BAE, 1). Critics tend to exaggerate for polemical reasons, Moratín says. They are, he insists in an aggressive metaphor, like bugs who wallow in the dark and filth instead of being like the bees that gather sweet honey; he obviously is referring to his own critics *(Poet,* 7; BAE, 8), who find a fault or two and blow it all out of proportion ("They strike out at my verses / Hiding away their own"). This, too, represents a slight change from the second poem he published. The sonnet "To the reader" expresses an offer to his readers to accept his poetry with its good, bad, and indifferent parts *(Poet,* 1; BAE, 17). Likewise, in the second issue *(Poet,* 2; BAE, 17) he seemed conciliatory as he attempted to reach a happy medium of theme, form, and style. Perhaps his audience took him too literally and informed him that there were, indeed, bad parts to his poetry.

Instead of turning to these know-nothing critics, Moratín exhorts his readers to read the great poets and to look for great models, some of which are to be found in Carlos III's court — Montiano will suffice as an example in both verse and drama *(Poet,* 5; BAE, 7). In the same vein, interspersed through all his verses are laudatory references to Anacreon, Homer, Virgil, Ovid, Cicero, and others, as well as direct imitation/translations of Marcial, Horace, and Pindar.[7] That these ancient masters have not only survived but prospered and remained exalted is sufficient proof for Nicolás that quality poetry is eternal. He counsels its study as a hedge against the ravages of time: he advises Dorisa that beauty and youth are ephemeral and only poetry remains undiminished by the passing of years. "Someone's beauty and her voice / And even wit and grace, / Are stolen by the flow of years / Leaving nothing in their place" *(Poet,* 4; BAE, 4). Time cannot destroy verses, he mistakenly thinks. He even adds patronizingly, in his faintly misogynistic manner, "The sciences are not impossible / For women to comprehend." He loved women, but he often misunderstood them. He returns to the commonplaces of Classical thought: wealth comes and goes, but the genius of poetry cannot be bought *(Poet,* 5; BAE, 6); men forget wealth and the wealthy, but lovers of the muses cherish poetry much longer. These may be truths, but they are also obvious examples of wishful thinking, and the lines have become a self-fulfilling prophecy: "When you've turned to ashes, / Both you and your purses, / Those who love the muses, / Will still love my verses" *(Poet,* 3; BAE, 6).

Another theme evident in the *Poet* is that of philosophical speculation on the state of the world, in which Moratín reveals his Classical bias; and on several points he even rejects the firmly held eighteenth-century belief that knowledge is power. While in most cases he upholds the value of knowledge (either for its own sake or, more frequently, as a tool to be employed for the betterment of society), he comments on its uselessness in stopping such natural phenomena as daybreak or the arrival of death *(Poet,* 2; BAE, 6). He even seems to contradict his own belief in the ability of social reformers to effect a transformation in society; man is not Rousseau's noble savage corrupted by civilization, he writes, but rather a being subjected to God's will:

Muchos que comer tienen
Pero no tienen ganas;
Otros están hambrientos
Y que comer les falta.
El tener uno y otro
No debo a herencia o trampa
Solo a Dios se lo debo;
A Dios pues doy las gracias. *(Poet,* 6; BAE, 6)

(Many people have much food
  But do not feel like eating;
  Others suffer hunger pangs
  And food is what they're needing.
  But to have one or the other
  I owe not to heredity or pranks,
  Only to God do I owe it,
  And to God I shall give thanks.)

The religious note is a minor one and will seldom reappear; Moratín did not put his faith in God alone, and we discover his gods to be, much in keeping with his empirical century, those which inhabited Parnassus. And this poem contradicts one written slightly earlier *(Poet,* 3; BAE, 17) in which he affirmed: "Let it be known that he alone is noble and honorable / Who shows himself through truth to be / Engendered solely by his own works." The concepts of knowledge ("science") and the tenuousness of life are not antithetical or, obviously, new. Moratín's philosophical stance is in many ways traditional, but always expressed in a sprightly and readable manner. Man's dangerous passions were a theme developed in his plays; in the *Poet* they metaphorically become a river in which man's existence is swept along.

Interestingly, these speculations are a minor part of his poetry. More evident and more convincingly real are his revelings in the sensuality of love, the importance of love, the exaltation of the *carpe diem* theme, and unconcern for death.

When medieval poets wrote of "gather ye rosebuds while ye may" they were reminding themselves to contemplate the rapidity of this life and to anticipate the rewards of the life beyond. Moratín throws off such ideas and displays the importance of living for the here and now. The key to this philosophy is the last strophe of a poem written in 1770 to Cadalso, and left unpublished until the *PW:* "Let's raise our cups up often / To whatever time is left us; / We'll dance a while and sing our songs, / And let death come to get us" (BAE, 7). The foreshadowings of the idea are clear in the *Poet* when he writes in honor of his own Saint's Day:

> Pues, huyan los pesares,
> Y baile mi Dorisa,
> Y venga la botella
> Del licor de Montilla.
> Y de arrayán y yedra
> La guirnalda me ciña
> La rubia sien, y luego
> Venga, venga mi lira.
> . . .
> Y pues su curso el tiempo
> No es posible reprima;
> Mientras viene la muerte,
> Gocemos de la vida. *(Poet,* 7; BAE, 7)

> (Well, have my troubles sent away,
>   And Dorisa in dance entwined,
>   And bring to me the bottle
>   Of sweet Montilla wine.
>   Of myrtle and of ivy
>   A garland please string on.
>   Yes, crown my brow, and then
>   Bring on my lyre, bring on.
>   . . .
>   And since it is that time's course
>   Cannot be delayed;
>   While death is coming on us,
>   Let's enjoy life while we may.)

Moratín's Epicurean roots are evident here, and the philosophy was one, as we have seen, that served him well not only in poetry, but also in life. The simple pleasures of love, friendship, and relative seclusion were a part of him, but only a part, for there battled within him the stoical belief that man needs to intervene in the affairs of society, to be a citizen of the world, and to respond to duty and reason. This latter concept is the intellectual substructure of his prose polemics and his plays, and it is not entirely absent from his poetry (see his "Spiritual Calm," *Poet,* 5; BAE, 38). So the battle between Moratín the Epicurean and Moratín the Stoic is a tense one, and the conflict is never fully resolved (the Dionysian aspect of his life and literature will become apparent when we study the *Whores' Art).*

His attitude toward death is less cavalier than the above-cited examples and more respectful in the elegies he wrote for the *Poet.* The demise of María Luisa, Archduchess of Austria and daughter of the powerful Duke of Parma, inspired a traditional elegy-cum-panegyric of little interest to us *(Poet,* 2; BAE, 25). More heartfelt was that which appeared in 1766, in the tenth number of the *Poet,* lamenting the death of Isabel de Farnesio. She had been like a mother to him ("I sing to my lady, to my mother" *Poet,* 10; BAE, 27). Her death brought forth an outpouring of 109 tercets in which his own pain is revealed. His emotions are external. He reacts personally, and very movingly, when addressing his beloved lady to "speak to you / For the last time." He remembers a loving past and feels in part that her death is a rejection, for there was a time when Isabel thought Moratín's poetry to be melodious; now "I was your swan: who would ever say / That I was then to sing your death?" He integrates (as he frequently does) a line from Garcilaso to underscore the great loss he feels. The poem is successful when he breaks from convention (the repetitious laments) and injects his very personal voice into it. Isabel was a mother to him, and he combines his role as son of his country with that of son of this noble lady.

Nevertheless, in the majority of his poems he values the pursuit of pleasure. Cupid had predicted that he would be a "Great poet / But a better lover" *(Poet,* 9; BAE, 2). Dorisa and the theme of love are frequent in the anacreontic odes and sonnets in the *Poet.* Her eyes and her voice — light and song — spin their web of enchantment around him, and he is entangled by it, if not entirely willingly. When Cupid fires his arrow, Moratín, "valiant," "arrogant," "insolent," and "proud," claims to resist the fatal blow as long as he can, until "It entered my heart: as a lover I now cry / . . . / Have pity on me, girl, for I adore you"*(Poet,* 2; BAE, 15). The power of love, a frustrating presence in his first poems to it, is seen as a negative force. Moratín considers himself too rational to be subverted by the treacheries of that chaotic sentiment, too thoughtful to be confused by such an unwanted presence. Yet the resistence is shortlived. Soon Flumisbo welcomes the seduction by Dorisa's song, readily mixing the heady sounds of her voice with the heady effects of wine *(Poet,* 2; BAE, 4–5). She affects him like sweet liquor *(Poet,* 5; BAE, 6) and his "cupidity" will come forth when encouraged both by the alcohol and by Dorisa. That desire apparently overtook him, for in a poem which he left out of the *Poet,* but which Leandro collected for the *PW* and which consequently reappeared in the BAE, Moratín found himself unable to remain faithful to his wife. The result was an intensely erotic poem reminiscent of the "Phyllis's Dove" series by Meléndez Valdés, when Moratín's touch no doubt concealed other contacts, either real or fantasized.

> Amor, tu que me diste los osados
> Intentos y la mano dirigiste,
> Y en el cándido seno la pusiste
> De Dorisa, en parajes no tocados;
> Si miras tantos rayos, fulminados
> De sus divinos ojos contra un triste,
> Dame el alivio, pues el daño huiste
> O acaben ya mi vida y mis cuidados.
> Apiádese mi bien. Dila que muero
> Del intenso dolor que me atormenta;
> Que si es tímido amor, no es verdadero;
> Que no es la audacia en el cariño afrenta,
> Ni merece castigo tan severo
> Un infeliz, que ser dichoso intenta. (BAE, 15)

> (Love, you who gave me the daring
>   Intentions, and who guided my hand,
>   And on the white breast of Dorisa
>   You put it, in places seldom touched;
>   If you see so many flashes, thundering
>   From her divine eyes against a sad man
>   Grant me solace, since you caused the pain,
>   Or end my life and these my cares.
>   Have pity on me. Tell her that I die
>   Of the intense hurt which torments me;
>   That if love is shy, it is not real;
>   That daring is not an insult when done with love
>   Nor does deserve such a severe punishment
>   An unhappy soul, who desires only joy.)

Her reaction to this act is evident in the poem, and Moratín deals with it in two poems which he did include in the *Poet,* different poems that carry similar titles ("To Dorisa's Scorn," *Poet,* 6; BAE, 15, and "Dorisa's Scorn," *Poet,* 7; BAE, 15). In the first, chastened by her temporary rejection, he illogically blames his love for her on none other than Dorisa: Why did you let me speak to you? Why did you let me see you? Why did you let "the passionate

fire of your heaven burn me''? he asks, while assuring her that his
constant love for her will follow her to the end of time. By the time
he wrote the second poem he seemed more apologetic, playing
upon her tenderness, his own insufferable pain, and his losing pre-
dicament: living with her scorn is impossible and yet not loving her
is unthinkable. In the interim between these two poems we note his
rationalization of their stormy period; he convinces himself that
true love of necessity demands heights of positive and negative
emotion. Other lovers who make claims of constant love and bliss,
who suffer no scorn, who feel no jealous pangs, who know nothing
except delicious happiness, know not true love either. They, at
least, know not the love of "such a beautiful lady" *(Poet,* 6; BAE,
15). The poem is his attempt to convince himself that their relations
are normal; it is a Valentine to Dorisa.

From the evidence published in the *Poet* we are not certain
whether his peace offering was successful or not. The remaining
poems to Dorisa detail either his continuing need to write about her
or the continuing sense of frustration he experienced because
of his love for her. We suspect it was rhetoric, for poems published later, although we cannot be certain of the dates of composition, reveal other and happier aspects of their relationship. She also
appears in a favorable light in his *Whores' Art,* which was written
later.

II *A Nearly Final Tally*

What was left out of the *Poet,* or written in the fourteen years between its last issue and Moratín's death, remained relatively unknown until Leandro's 1821 edition of his father's works. By then
the star of Neoclassicism had waned, and Spain was preparing itself
for new currents, most notably that of Romanticism. But Nicolás's
verses had much to say to Spaniards in the 1820s, especially those
whose educations had been Classical (and that included almost
every educated Spaniard). His greatest impact, however, took place
while he was writing and reading his poems — that is, in the late
1760s and 1770s. Even though no edition appeared during his lifetime, we do know that Leandro said he was preparing a manuscript
for publication in the late 1770s. Whether this is true or not (and we
have reason to believe that it was more likely said to deflect suspicion that he had retouched many of his father's poems prior to
their publication in 1821), Nicolás no doubt continued to write

poems. Leandro's collection is the rest of Nicolás's short poetry and it contains some of his best writings.

The *Posthumous Works (PW)* contains in several instances significantly different renditions of poems which originally appeared in the *Poet,* and it is these new versions that eventually were reprinted in the BAE. Two hypotheses come to mind: either Nicolás had second thoughts about some of his poems and he was revising them as Leandro claims (he says the manuscript was given to Bernascone), or another hand retouched the poems prior to their appearance in 1821. We cannot be sure which of these two suggestions is correct, but since we do know that Leandro was in the habit of "correcting" his father's poetry (we shall deal with this later), it is not unlikely that many changes can be attributed to the son. Nicolás wrote very rapidly and seldom looked back on his own works.

A full look at Moratín's poems confirms the importance of the themes and structures that appeared in the *Poet:* poetry, humor, and Dorisa dominate in the *PW,* with the addition of some of the epic and heroic themes that he claimed then he would eschew. The Dorisa poems are of particular interest for their grace and beauty. These poems to Dorisa are richer in emotion and visual imagery than the earlier ones were. They display the same ebb and flow in their relationship, and Moratín's reactions to them, but with a clearer eroticism than before. The spirit of Erato predominates as Moratín enlists her aid in "The Dream" *(PW,* 67-71; BAE, 2), where she bends to kiss him passionately, thereby inflaming a passion which only "the laughter / of my Dorisa" can contain. The setting is an idyllic pastoral one taken not from Flumisbo's dreams but from his experience — the Arlas river in the Alcarria region is the location of his mother's family home, where he often retreated for summer visits. Presumably his days spent there were pastoral enough, but not erotic and certainly not enhanced by the presence of Dorisa. His memory served him well when combined with his fantasies, and, as we know, those fantasies were not always fulfilled. Many of these new poems display his sense of rejection when Dorisa was scornful or coquettish *(PW,* 77-78, BAE, 15-16; *PW,* 1, BAE, 16; *PW,* 172-73, BAE, 16; *PW,* 160-61, BAE, 16). She was after all a lady of the theater, emotional herself and perhaps worldly-wise. The suggestion in the *Poet* that their relationship was a stormy one is confirmed in these later poems.

Moratín's real style is displayed in those numerous poems celebrating Dorisa. Dorisa as a shepherd's companion, Dorisa's song, Dorisa's body, Dorisa's marvelous clothes, and above all, Dorisa's glorious eyes — those eyes that become part of him and illuminate his existence, control him, and both weaken and strengthen him. "Look, Love said with a smile full of lies / I have more than enough power to control you; / And he pointed to Dorisa's eyes" *(PW, 8-9; BAE, 15)*. Inspired by Petrarch's Sonnet 39, Flumisbo writes:

> Bendita sea la hora, el año, el día,
> Y la ocasión, y el venturoso instante,
> En que rendí mi corazón amante
> A aquellos ojos donde Febo ardía.
> Bendito el esperar, y la porfía
> Y el alto empeño de mi fe constante,
> Y las saetas y el arco fulminante
> Con que abrasó Cupido el alma mía.
> Bendita la aflicción que he tolerado
> En las cadenas de mi dulce dueño,
> Y los suspiros, llantos y esquiveces,
> Los versos que a su gloria he consagrado
> Y han de vencer el duro tiempo el ceño,
> Y ella bendita innumerables veces. *(PW, 130-31; BAE, 16)*

> (Blessed the hour, the year, the day,
>   And the occasion, and the lucky instant
>   In which I gave over my lover's heart
>   To those eyes where Phoebus burned.
>   Blessed the waiting, and the disputes
>   And the perseverence of my own constant faith,
>   And the arrows and the thundering bow
>   With which Cupid captured my soul.
>   Blessed the pains that I have tolerated
>   Enchained by my eversweet mistress,
>   And the sighs, tears, and disdain,
>   The verses which I have made to her glory
>   And which will conquer an eon's revenge,
>   And her, blessed innumerable times.)

Moratín gently conveys his seduction by Dorisa's eyes, and she comes alive for us. Dorisa may be "modest," "honest," and "timid" *(PW, 54; BAE, 16)*, as her lover depicts her, but she is also luscious, and he hungers for her. In Sonnet 11 the pretext is the description of her costumed in a "magnificent dress," but Moratín produces another subtly erotic piece, ripe with descriptions of the body on which the dress is draped. The second strophe reads: "What a beautiful breast, where love its seat / Has placed, and from there it strikes the lovers / Absorbed in watching its elegant / Form, its delicious movement!" With shattering and lusty irony he concludes: "What heroic and noble thoughts I have!" *(PW,* 156; BAE, 16). Even in their periods of difficulty Dorisa is as seductive as always. He calls her a "monster of ingratitude and of beauty" *(PW,* 156; BAE, 16) revealing his own difficult adjustment to the ups and downs of their relationship. If Leandro respected the order of his father's verses, then we may learn something from the first page of the *PW,* where Nicolás protests the thanklessness of Dorisa, who, contrary to Nature, which responds to the poet's laments, refuses to bear witness to the unhappiness she reportedly causes him.

This warning note appears only in the sonnets, and on balance we discover that the painful side of love frequently gives way to the carefree, joyous side. If Dorisa can be scornful and distant, she can also be playful and gay. The lightness of the anacreontic odes attests to this positive aspect of their love affair. Moratín strikes a relaxed tone, befitting the poetic form which he chooses, and permits the Epicureanism of his poetic personality to dominate his thoughts. "Few in years / And of graces many / Alone and blessed / She was singing" *(PW,* 161–68; BAE, 2–3); she becomes an elusive vision who blended with Nature to enchant the poet (in the area near Pastrana once again). Out there, away from the hustle-bustle of the capital, Moratín sheds his pomp and pedantry, claiming (falsely, naturally, but attractively) to embrace the farmer's life:

> Hoy mi Dorisa
> Se va a la aldea,
> Pues se recrea,
> Viendo trillar.
> Sígola aprisa:
> Cuantos placeres,
> Mantua, tuvieres,
> Voy a olvidar.
> Que yo no quiero
> Más dignidades:
> Las vanidades
> Me quitó Amor.
> Ni fama espero,

Ni anhelo a nada;
Sólo me agrada
Ser labrador. *(PW,* 46–48; BAE, 4)

(Today my Dorisa
  Goes to the village,
  She watches the silage
  And watches them reap.
  I follow her quickly:
  Madrid's many pleasures
  Are old-fashioned treasures
  Which I shall not keep.
  I no longer want
  The public's attention
  A useless dimension
  Which Love took from me.
  For fame I seek not.
  I have few desires;
  I only aspire
  A farmer to be.)

So pleasure was to be his, and, in a poem that could stand as his epitaph, he pays homage to the glories of friendship, the headiness of good wine, and the intense pleasure of being near his beloved. The poem which begins "Hoy celebro los días / De mi dulce poeta" (the first poem extracted in this chapter) synthesizes these concerns. It goes on to reveal: "We'll raise our voices in happy toast / Until we lose our minds / In the cups brimming over / With the sweet and scented wine." His lyricism, his Epicurean abandon, and his open acceptance of life culminate in the almost hedonistic last lines of the poem.

The theme appears in other poems, as do praises of womanly virtues. He makes several attempts at humor, satire, and philosophical musings, ending up at times only with empty pronouncements. He is generous in his praise of his friends: Conti, Bernascone, Count Aranda, Gabriel de Borbón, Ceballos, Signorelli, and the Duke of Medinasidonia all receive his lush and well-written verses concerning their successes (Conti after his excellent translation of Garcilaso's First Eclogue in 1771, Aranda as General Captain of Castile, Gabriel for his heroic war effort in Morocco, Signorelli upon publication of his 1777 *Critical History* — to which Moratín contributed — etc.). As we have come to expect, the manuscript of the Ceballos poem is very different, and longer, than the one Leandro published *(PW,* 93–97; BAE, 22).[8] Although Flumisbo insisted in the *Poet* that he would not write of heroic things, he finally wrote five very good and very lively ballads that treated precisely heroic themes. In these poems we detect the enthusiasm, the eye for local color, and the interest in Spanish history and heroes that he again pulled together while writing the famous "Bullfight Festival in Madrid." Still, it was Dorisa and the love theme which formed the nucleus of his poems written after the early *Poet,* and which, while unfortunately little known today, establish him as one of the best poets of his day. Dorisa's death in 1772 produced a tender and anguished ode on her "absence" *(PW,* 49–52; BAE, 35–36), but gradually, sadder and with a sense of irreplaceable loss, he turned to other matters.

III *Moratín, Bullfight Fan*

Moratín was one of the few enlightened writers who actively supported and defended the bullfight. Feijoo had argued against it, as did Campomanes. Jovellanos opposed it on moral, historical, social, and economic grounds. Nicolás's friends Tomás de Iriarte and Cadalso (who called it a barbarity) refused to share his enthusiasm.[9] Even Clavijo, Nicolás's friend and ally, was horrified by the waste of bulls and horses which the fight invariably produced. One of the few intellectuals who had demonstrated any admiration for the fight had been Juan de Iriarte, one of Moratín's first acquaintances when he arrived in Madrid in 1759. *Taurimachia matritensis* (The Art of Bullfighting in Madrid) had originally appeared in 1725, but a reprinted version came out in Iriarte's selected works in 1774. With few exceptions current theories as to its social value were not in agreement with Moratín's enthusiastic acceptance of this special sport/drama.[10] It was, in his iconoclastic view, a spectacle which "only in Spain was not barbaric."[11] He set down his thoughts on the subject in an interesting letter to Prince Pignatelli on July 25, 1776,[12] written perhaps in response to Campomanes's denouncement of the sport in his *Discurso sobre la educación popular de los artesanos y su fomento* (Discourse on the Popular Education of Artesans and Its Improvement; Madrid, 1775).

Moratín's "Carta histórica sobre el origen y progresos de la fiesta de toros en España" (Historical Letter Concerning the Origin and Advances of the Bullfight in Spain) was published in

1777 and announced in the *Gaceta de Madrid* on July 15. It is a prose compilation of opinion, muddled facts, and history. In it, Moratín attempts a historical overview of the bullfight, citing its development on the Iberian Peninsula. Its value is less for the historical data (some of it totally wrong, such as introducing the Cid as the country's first bullfighter, an error also made in the "Bullfight Festival in Madrid") than for the information on the contemporary bullfight that he offers. While discussing the fate of this diversion in the eighteenth century, he relates the activities of several famed fighters, a couple of whom were his intimate friends. The dominant note in the letter, as we are not surprised to learn, is patriotic: he claims that it was "the ferocity of the bulls which Spain raised . . . plus the bravery of the Spaniards" (BAE, 141) that engendered this unique pastime. His own interest was strictly as a spectator, but he does state that his maternal grandfather had a reputation as a good amateur participant in the Alcarria region. His friend and mentor Medinasidonia's great grandfather also is singled out for praise.

His sources for this letter were varied: his own memory, those of his friends and relatives (his father, still alive in 1776, was apparently recalling scenes from his own youth), gossip and anecdote, as well as several texts which he specifically mentions: Francisco de Cepeda, *Resumpta Historial de España* (Historical Review of Spain); Gaspar Bonifaz, *Reglas de torear* (Rules of Bullfighting); Luis de Trejo, *Obligaciones y duelo* (Duties and Duels); Juan de Valencia, *Advertencias para torear* (Advice for Bullfighting); Gregorio de Tapia y Salcedo, *Ejercicios para la jineta* (Riding Drills); Diego de Torres, *Reglas de torear;* and Nicolás Rodrigo Noveli, *Cartilla de torear* (A Primer of Bullfighting). Along with these treatises on the subject, he alludes to Góngora, Jerónimo de Salas Barbadillo, Juan de Yangüe, and Lope, from whose *Jerusalén* he offers a brief quotation. Of course, the treatise's lasting worth resides in the fact that the eighteenth century's greatest painter produced a series of masterly etchings based on it: Francisco de Goya, who arrived in Madrid four years after the publication of Moratín's "Historical Letter," read it with great interest and his extraordinary *Tauromaquia* series began as detailed illustrations of it.[13] We also know that Goya personally received a copy of Nicolás's *PW* from Leandro's friend Juan Antonio Melón in 1823.[14]

Goya was not the only artist impressed with Moratín's pamphlet:

Mariano José de Larra, that exquisite writer who hovered between the aesthetics of Neoclassicism and the metaphysics of Romanticism, used the "Historical Letter" as the basis for his discussion of the bullfight in an early article published in his *Duende satírico* (Satirical Goblin). José Escobar has studied the influence (a near plagiarism) with impressive rigor.[15]

Leandro means to scandalize and to charm us with the following story concerning the attraction of one of his grandfather's servants to the bullfight, but we can imagine the secret glee that the episode produced in Nicolás:

It was Monday; and wishing that I take a stroll and amuse myself, he called Juan, an old Asturian servant that he had, and he charged him to take me to the Retiro Park, where I could entertain myself tossing crumbs to the fish in the pond there, for which he provided us with a large chunk of bread. We returned from our task somewhat late; my grandparents were worried; and to the various questions which they asked me, I responded that it had been very pleasant; that there were many people, shouts, whistling, and hubbub; that the fish came out one by one; and the men, some mounted on horseback, jabbed them in the neck with long spears; that others ran them through with swords; and when they fell dead, mules came out and dragged them out of the pond. Not much else was needed to figure out that Juan had taken a different road, and instead of taking me to see the fish, had entertained me at a bullfight.[16]

A. *"Fiesta de toros en Madrid"*

The apotheosis of Moratín's love for the bullfight resides in what has become his most famous poem. Spanish schoolchildren still memorize sections of it. The series of *quintillas* (stanzas of five octosyllabic lines) entitled "La fiesta de toros en Madrid" (Bullfight Festival in Madrid) has been called one of "the most important compositions of the eighteenth century"[17] and, more recently, "the most famous *[quintilla]* in the Spanish language."[18] On this last point there appears to be no argument, and the praises the poem has received attest to its continued popularity among critics and general readers.

The controversy concerns its authorship and the influence of Leandro, whose penchant for "correcting" his father's verses has caused not a little gnashing of teeth. The published version of the poem and the manuscript version are different. The manuscript in question belonged to Fernando José de Velasco, one of the prestigious members of the Council of Castile, who, according to Aureliano Fernández Guerra, received it directly from Moratín himself in 1773. The academic positions are these: Leandro included a version of it in the 1821 *PW*. Quintana, who reprinted it in his *Selected Spanish Poems* of 1830, stated that Leandro had reworked the poem substantially before bringing it to light in 1821, yet he nevertheless published what he suspected to be a truncated version. Fernández Guerra,[19] writing in 1883, rejected Quintana's charge, claiming instead that Nicolás corrected it before he died. He in turn has been challenged by arguments put forth by Fernando Lázaro Carreter,[20] whose position is that Leandro retouched the poem, improving it in the process. It is generally agreed today that Leandro did rewrite and condense much of the "Bullfight Festival," although there is not a clear consensus on which version is better. J. L. Alborg, while suspecting that the reworked version is by Leandro, nevertheless encourages us to judge Nicolás's poetic accomplishments by this second version, simply because it is the "official" one.[21] When we know the longer version to be Nicolás's, and admit to the dubious authorship of the reworked version, such a position is surprising and untenable.

The original, that of Nicolás, published by Fernández Guerra, is a richly detailed and somewhat diffuse series of 158 *quintillas* that portray an incident which supposedly took place in eleventh-century Madrid. The hero: the Cid. The place: Madrid, that "noble castle." The time: the feast day of the city's Moorish ruler, Alimenon. The original *quintillas* are much more leisurely than Leandro's condensed version,[22] and they are replete with more description of the setting and of the individuals involved in the celebration. The same leisurely pace is evident in Moratín's rendition of "Cortés's Ships Destroyed," as we shall soon see.

Moratín first presents the place, the purpose, and the main participants in the action of the poem (strophes 1–2), including the beautiful Moorish princess Elipa (3), and then provides a lavish description of the city and its Moorish inhabitants, all bedecked for the festivities (6–14, 17–18). The handsome men display their bravery (15–16) and the pretty ladies come from miles around with their lovers to enjoy the day (19–33). It is this latter section which Cossío sees, perhaps too generously, as having been inspired by Lope's *La hermosura de Angélica* (Angelica's Beauty), but Moratín's is so much richer and more detailed that if any influence existed it was more indirect, following a traditional narrative pattern, than direct. The bull is only briefly mentioned (32) before Moratín brings Elipa back into the scene (34) and subtly links her with the other prize to be won that day, the bull itself (35). More resplendent description follows as Flumisbo adds to the lively color and Arabic ambience, not forgetting to lay before us the bravery of the men who are anxious to prove themselves in battle against this noble beast (36–43). The bull is ferocious, wild, and fearsome; it maims and kills while refusing to be subjugated by its human adversaries (44–61), and Moratín's descriptions of it are brilliantly alive. Many men are defeated — even Aliatar loses one of his best steeds to a mortal blow by this dangerous beast; no one dares to face it until the gatekeeper announces the arrival of a stranger, a Christian (62–63).

Elipa nods her permission to let this "gallant gentleman" enter. Who is he? (64–79). The reader's first clue comes in the form of a catch-phrase, "nunca mi espada tal venciera" (my sword shall not be conquered), a line which popular balladry associated with the Cid. His very presence suggests strength and grace (80–88), and the crowd responds to his courageous air and his youth (89–91). A handmaiden of Elipa tells her who he is and, recognizing him, they discuss his past deeds (92–101). Here, about two-thirds of the way through the poem, Moratín intercalates a patriotic harangue, breaking his narrative flow in favor of an anachronistic discussion of the kings which followed the Cid's lord, Alfonso VI, and the imperative nature of regaining Madrid for Christianity (102–13). Leandro wisely left this entire section out of his version. Elipa had spoken to this Christian gentleman before, secretly (114), and he in turn recognizes her, courteously bowing to her in respect (115–20), and eliciting additional musings from Moratín on the Cid's fame (121–24). The crowd murmurs with wonder and enthusiasm (125), and the core of the poem — the battle between the Cid and the crazed and brutal animal — arrives.

The bull stares (127); the Cid responds (128), placing himself carefully where Elipa can enjoy the fight (129). The battle is enjoined with rapid action and increasing tension (130–36), and Elipa becomes worried (137). As the fight rages on the Cid gradually gains the upper hand and finally succeeds in killing the brute (138–41). The crowd erupts in jubilant cheering (142), which is magnified as the Cid offers the prize he has conquered to the lady Elipa (143–45). Her acceptance (146–48) fires up the jealousy of Aliatar, who insults the Cid and challenges him to battle (149–51).

Naturally, the Christian hero accepts and the city is nearly plunged into vicious battle between the opposing sides (152–53) when the arrival of Christian troops (154–57) enables the Cid to extricate himself from the situation and to swear to recapture Madrid for Christianity (158). This cheap-shot arrival of friendly troops is the same weak ploy that Moratín used to "solve" the conflicts established in his plays *Lucretia* and *Hormesinda*. It weakened the dramas, and its effect on this poem is no different.

Nevertheless, it is Moratín's enthusiasm for the colorful Moorish celebrations and his obvious attraction to the challenge ●f the bullfight that beckon us to this lovely poem. His *quintillas* flow smoothly in a cascade of colors, sizes, shapes, and action. We get the impression that his haste forced him to choose trite or repetitious words or phrases lacking poetic impact, but our interest in the poem's story enables us to overlook such weaknesses. The major fault in Nicolás's version is not its easy flow or its length but the jarring intercalation that seems too artificial, too out of place.

Flumisbo's direct sources for this poem are two: Salas Barbadillo's "La patrona de Madrid" (The Patron Saint of Madrid, 1609), and Lope's "Isidro." A new edition of the Salas poem appeared in Madrid in 1750, and many similarities with it appear in the "Bullfight Festival." Moratín read Salas, as the "Historical Letter" proves. The forms of the two poems are very different, as are the general intent and actions, and except for a reference to Madrid as a "strong castle" in Salas's first Book, it is not until Books 8 and 9 (strophes 471–514) that we encounter strong points of contact. Madrid "burns in festivals" for the king of Toledo's birthday; the bullring bursts with colorful Moorish finery and beautiful maidens; the fierce bull charges into the ring, bathed in sweat; Aliatar is the mayor of Madrid, etc. The tone of Moratín's poem is so similar that a direct inspiration cannot be ignored, although it is hardly "copied" from Salas, as Castrovido suggests.[23] From Lope, Moratín absorbed additional ambience, the *quintilla* form, and assorted technical details.

The question has been raised as to the sources of Moratín's knowledge of Arabic customs and artifacts. Both Fernández Guerra[24] and Alonso Cortés[25] refute the supposition that Moratín had before him a written work on the subject (the manuscript in the Biblioteca Nacional calls the poem a "translation of an Arabic piece that Mariano Pizzi gave him"). What he did have was the friendship of Pizzi, who was a professor of Arabic in the Imperial

College and finally a colleague of Moratín when the latter substituted in Ayala's chair. Pizzi was also an intimate of the San Sebastián Inn, and surely Moratín and he discussed the details of Arabic jewelry, dress, names, and festivities while Moratín was composing the poem.

Leandro refused to overlook those elements that he considered to be superfluous or unpoetical. Gone is the "apostrophe," for which we give him due credit; but also gone are eighty-six of his father's original *quintillas*. The resulting poem, while strictly and academically speaking a "purer" poem, does an injustice to Moratín's festive concept. A statistical table of the changes looks like this:

Version	Strophes	Verses	Strophes Eliminated	Verses Changed
(1770s)	158	790	—	—
1821	72	360	86	137

Leandro succeeds in tightening it up, cutting away many descriptive passages without losing the plotline, and selecting words that fit better into the rhythmic structure. He eliminates a strophe that Moratín had carelessly included twice (40, 53), and transposes another to fit his conception of the poem's argument (114). These strophes disappear: 3-5, 7-15, 17-18, 20, 22, 24-25, 27-31, 33, 35-41, 43, 46, 51-54, 58-59, 65-69, 71, 74-77, 81-82, 84, 86, 88, 97-100, 102-15, 117-20, 122-24, 128-29, 131, 132, 138, 146, and 153. As can be seen, the majority of the cuts are from the first half of the poem (plus the "apostrophe"), where Moratín was busy creating his gala scenes. "Elipa" is now "Zaida," a change which Fernández Guerra applauds; it certainly was a more common Arabic name, but it was also more commonplace. In fact, many of Fernández Guerra's opinions were solely personal preferences, and his claims that this or that word was infinitely better in the second version merely reflected his attempt to prove that the changes were Nicolás's own. Not everyone agrees.

All of the other strophes, with very few exceptions, undergo Leandro's redesign of a word, a phrase, or the entire *quintilla*. Gone are anachronisms such as mentions of the Order of Santiago (not yet founded in the Cid's time) or the confusing of clothing materials and styles not yet in vogue. Gone are two references that, while Leandro might have considered them inappropriate to the poem, were typical of his father's art: a mention of Arenal Street in

Madrid (67) and a reference to the goddess of love, Venus (121), who figures so prominently in *The Whores' Art*. In fact, in light of Nicolás's penchant for almost geographical descriptions of his beloved city, we are surprised that there are not more such scenes in this poem. What Leandro gains in poetic precision he loses in realistic ambience; the absence of Nicolás's frequent Arabic artifacts and names pulls the poem away from its intended exoticism and places it onto nearly neutral ground.

Some changes by Leandro are just that, changes that neither add to nor detract from Nicolás's work. Leandro's lovely *quintilla* 9 replaces his father's *quintilla* 32, which dramatically combines the three elements in the approaching action — the spectators, the brave fighters, and the caged bulls, waiting to unleash their energy into the ring. Leandro eliminates completely *quintilla* 35, which subtly combines the two objects of the men's passions — Elipa, the desirable lady, and the ferocious bull. The symbolism of the male/female dichotomy linked with the traditional dialectic of active vs. passive disappears at Leandro's insistence, and thus one of the key features of the poem is diluted. Nicolás's knack for strong alliteration, which Tomás de Iriarte would make fun of several years later, was even strengthtened by Leandro. Where Nicolás was content with "Arrancó desde el *t*oril / Y a *T*arfe *t*iró por *t*ierra" (47), Leandro rewrites it as "Salió un *t*oro del *t*oril / Y a *T*arfe *t*iró por *t*ierra" (14). Still, it is not Leandro's poem but rather his father's, and the changes are of style, not of substance. Leandro takes the poem from its popular roots and gives it to the academies.

Whether in Nicolás's version or Leandro's, the poem remains one of the outstanding narrative poems of the Enlightenment; I. L. McClelland is right on the mark when she writes that "Moratín's artistry is wholly triumphant."[26] Cossío recognizes its importance as a transitional link between the Moorish literature of the Renaissance and the interest in Moorish themes exhibited during the Romantic period by such great poets as Rivas and Zorrilla.[27] Moratín's attraction to the exotic Orient could be designated one of the aspects of Romanticism (pre-Romanticism?) that began to appear in the 1770s, and although Moratín's frame of mind was clearly not Romantic, Peers does not hesitate to write that his verses "foreshadow" those of the Romantic age,[28] a thought that echoed Menéndez Pelayo's more forceful characterization of Moratín's "entirely Spanish and Romantic poetic genius."[29] J. H. Mundy argues that Moratín's poem influenced several poems by

Juan Artolas,[30] and examples abound of his impact on other poets, from the already-mentioned Romantics through the forgotten Pedro Viñolas (who penned a short "lyric episode" based on Moratín's *quintillas*[31]), and even on to Machado and García Lorca.

Moratín's descriptions are realistic, fully within the Spanish epic and narrative poetic tradition dating as far back as the prototypical Cid poem, the *Poem of the Cid*. This tradition, however, bypasses some of those poets who are Moratín's major inspirations: the interest of Garcilaso, Herrera, and Fray Luis in the bullfight is nonexistent. Conversely, that of Lope is notorious and Moratín becomes the eighteenth century's greatest exponent of interests developed by, among others, that very Lope.[32] This is another example of our inability to consider Moratín as an enemy of Lope, a thought which is as widely repeated as it is inaccurate. Lázaro Carreter is correct when he writes: "There was a great deal in the Madrilenian Moratín of his countryman Lope . . . once again, and more clearly than ever, the detractor of our theater unites with the nationalistic poetic past."[33]

B. *Pedro Romero*

Moratín's other composition that is universally credited with being among the best of his century is the ode "To Pedro Romero, Remarkable Bullfighter" (BAE, 56–57). It is an exquisite piece, full of the same lively action and intense love of the fight that Moratín had already displayed. It is also a superb paean of praise to an outstanding practitioner of that art. It is stately and restrained. It was not known in Nicolás's own times except perhaps by a few of his friends. Leandro first published it in 1821 *(PW,* 99–104), and Quintana thought it good enough to include in his *Selected Spanish Poems* of 1830 (volume 4, 55–59). This short but powerful poem is another perspective on Moratín's well-documented attraction for the celebration of the bullfight, the pitting of beast against man in a noble fight to the death. The Moorish and popular ambience of the "Historical Letter" and the "Bullfight Festival" has given way to the Classical world of gods and allegorical (yes, allegorical) beings. Couched in the structure of a Pindaric ode in 120 verses, the poem begins in traditional and trite strophes that employ overblown exhortations to the "golden zither of Apollo" and the "sacred muse," begging them to raise their song and voice to the heavens in celebration. Yet it takes Moratín only eight verses to catch his stride and to ground his imagery in terms of his subject by linking the Classical sounds with those made by the screaming multitudes in the "bloody Madrilenian bullring, / In whose arena the conquering artist / Fearlessly stands firm / Filled with glory which fame sings forth." The ring fills with admirers bedecked in their rich adornments. The action begins as the hero, never named in the body of the poem, comes into focus.

The "brave youth" surveys the plaza, his "handsome face" gazing with pride; this Achilles, this Jason, enjoins the battle serenely. In a masterly stroke, Moratín switches narrative voices in the fourth strophe, trading in the third person for the second, thereby personalizing the action and bringing the reader into the tension of the fight. He addresses a singular and familiar "you," and we immediately identify with the hero. "You wait for it . . . "

> Horror pálido cubre los semblantes,
> En trasudor bañados,
> Del atónito vulgo silencioso;
> Das a las tiernas damas mil cuidados
> Y envidia a sus amantes:
> Todo el concurso atiende pavoroso
> El fin de este dudoso
> Trance. La fiera que llamó el silbido
> A ti corre veloz, ardiendo en ira,
> Y amenazando mira
> El rojo velo al viento suspendido.
> Da tremendo bramido,
> Como el toro de Fálaris ardiente,
> Hácese atrás, resopla, cabecea,
> Eriza la ancha frente,
> La tierra escarba y larga cola ondéa. (BAE, 37)

> (Pale horror covers the faces,
>   Bathed in perspiration,
>   Of the silent, astonished mob,
>   You cause anxiety in the ladies
>   And envy in their lovers:
>   The crowd awaits with dread
>   The end to this uncertain
>   Peril. The beast, his attention gained,
>   Charges you quickly, with burning hate,
>   And menacing watches
>   The red veil suspended in the wind.
>   It issues forth a dreadful roar,

> Like the burning bull of Phalaris,[34]
> It retreats, snorts, lifts up its head,
> Bristles that broad forehead,
> Scratches the earth, and swings its lengthy tail.)

The accumulation of verbs heightens the drama by making the danger seem imminent. The bull is alive, fierce, shrewd, and rapid, but the fight ends quickly, with the "impetuous brute / Dead at your feet." Ever the patriot, Moratín lifts Romero's success to a higher level, comparing his daring to that of all the sons of Spain, willing to protect their king and their nation against any and all enemies. He makes a telling point, based more on rhetoric than recent history, when he notices that any nation which produces men brave enough to do battle with those frightening beasts produces men bold enough to do battle with anything. What was surprising about Moratín's poem was that he had the audacity to hold up for Classical worship a mere bullfighter, whose profession was hardly respected, let alone admired. Moratín praises the skill in terms more generally reserved for gods, kings, and military heroes.

Pedro Romero was not Moratín's invention, but a well-known bullfighter descended from a line of bullfighters, most notably the famous Juan Romero. Born in Ronda in 1754, Pedro gained fame as a young man, a fame which Moratín followed and helped to propagate in his "Historical Letter." Moratín considered this new bullfighter "to have raised this art to such perfection that the imagination cannot perceive how it is capable of any advancement whatsoever."[35] Pedro's greatest skill was his calm approach to the kill, which he carried out with delicate artistry. Goya, often attracted to the same subjects as Moratín, painted his portrait, and his largess was later documented by other authors (Somoza, Estebánez Calderón), as Cossío points out.[36] Larra valued the poem enough to reprint it in the previously cited issue of *El Duende Satírico*. Even Lord Byron, who often sought inspiration in Spanish sources, was impressed by the poem and plagiarized it (without giving any credit to Moratín) in the First Canto of *Childe Harold's Pilgrimage*, particularly in stanzas 74–79.

C. *Moratín and the Bullfight*

Moratín's genius was to transform bullfight literature from a mere pastime or bright ambience placed into literary works for local color to serious literature, worthy of attention and study in its own right. His attraction to the bullfight was complete and early,[37] and his literary rendering of that attraction resulted in two poems regarded as among the finest not only of his endeavors but also of the entire eighteenth century's. The theme appears and reappears in many of his works, including the scabrous *Whores' Art,* where he combines the bullring with the Classical amphitheater in the same manner as he did in the ''Ode to Pedro Romero'' (Cossío demonstrates that Luzán was among the first to make this connection[38]). In the same vein, and much more shockingly, he combines the imagery of lovemaking and bullfighting by counseling young men to imitate the bullfighter Cándido, who ''lunges'' his sword cleanly and quickly,[39] an idea which he repeats and develops in the *Whores' Art.*

The theme of bullfighting was one of the four permitted at the San Sebastián Inn gatherings. His enthusiasm for it in the face of organized opposition was manifest, and he refused to betray that enthusiasm. Through his writings Moratín gave new life to the fight as a national and popular art form just as his son's friend Goya gave it a graphic reality. The eighteenth century witnessed a transformation in the style, conduct, and appreciation of the bullfight, and Moratín can easily take credit for helping to effect that transformation.

IV El arte de las putas: *Flumisbo's Floozies*

On the surface, *El arte de las putas* (The Whores' Art) is so very different from Moratín's other poetic endeavors that we are left breathless by its scandalous crudeness. Yet substantively it is very much the work of Moratín and very much in keeping with the other works we have been discussing. The bold scabrousness is new, as is the lusty titillation of this tour through Madrid's back streets, yet we immediately recognize in it traits of Moratín's other poems: the intense attachment to Madrid, the personal (even autobiographical) flavor, the rich and colorful details, the heavy borrowing from Spanish literature, and the easy flow of verses. Moratín's delight in the opposite sex insinuated itself into his life (Dorisa) and his poetry. Apart from the *Whores' Art,* he has a short ode entitled ''All Girls Deserve'' *(PW,* 2; BAE, 5) which lists his delight in brunettes, blondes, girls with dark eyes, girls with blue eyes, and so on, and ends with a tongue-in-cheek comment: ''That's why all girls /

Are able to enchant me; / And don't you see what a reasonable / And prudent man I am?''

The Whores' Art was never published in Moratín's lifetime, although it was widely circulated in manuscript and most likely read, in part at least, at the tertulia at San Sebastián. What his wife thought of it, if she saw it at all, we can only imagine. Tomás de Iriarte alludes to it in a series of satirical verses, writing of Moratín,

> que a Hormesinda y a Guzmán
> cantó en lenguaje morisco,
> y por maestro de un Arte
> muy semejante al de Ovidio
> ha visto inmortalizados
> sus versos . . . . [40]

> (who sang of Hormesinda and Guzmán
> in a Moorish tongue,
> and who, as author of an Art
> very similar to Ovid's
> has seen his verses
> immortalized . . . .)

and the *Index* mentions its prohibition as early as June 20, 1777.[41] A printed version appeared 118 years after Moratín's death, edited anonymously and based on a manuscript copied in 1813 by one Laurent Falcon in Valladolid.[42] Its appearance in 1898 no doubt sent shivers of horror up the spine of Menéndez Pelayo, whose response to it (and he refused even to mention its title) was the following: "It is one of the clearest, most repugnant and shameless examples of the antisocial and antihuman virus that boiled at the core of empirical and sensualist philosophy, of utilitarian morals, and of the theory of pleasure."[43] Recently two critical editions have appeared,[44] in essence the first ones to reach a potentially wide public, since the 1898 edition was a very limited one (the editor claims that only fifty copies were printed). This is one work that Leandro did not amend; in fact he did not even mention it in his *Life* of his father.

Nicolás was the author of the poem, as the last lines make clear: " . . . of such a grand art / The great Corsair, the practical and skilled, / The sweet Moratín was my teacher" (192). He would have us believe that this poem, written in 1,995 verses in four cantos (it is his second-longest poem), is "didactic," and certainly there is a lesson to be learned from the adventures that he describes in it. It is also, however, surprisingly autobiographical: Dorisa, his beloved songstress, is mentioned several times; the Madrid of the poem is Moratín's city, detailed with the same enthusiastic observation as we have seen elsewhere; and the thematic and stylistic elements all point to the suspicion that the poem is more than an academic exercise in morality. One of the strongest notes is the author's horror of contracting venereal disease, a very personal note since we have reason to believe that Moratín died at the age of forty-two of that dreaded infirmity. His penchant for skirt-chasing has been long suspected, and the evidence provided in Leandro's diary indicates that he, like his father, patronized the prostitutes of Madrid's back streets. Leandro alludes to a certain Liarta,[45] who may be the same "young girl" whom Nicolás mentions in the *Art* (143.). Nicolás also personalizes his involvement when he mentions Belica, a known disease carrier, by writing: "Oh, Belica!, your grace and beauty; / Public opinion lies when it says / That your love is tastefully homicidal" (142). But it was true, for Jovellanos, who got the story either from common gossip or directly from Moratín's poem, later wrote: "But he learned to fear the love of Belica / The venomous, in whose sweet arms / More than one young man gave his last sigh."[46] Moratín confesses to having had contact with Belica (187); perhaps she was the cause of his own case of venereal disease. If so, his words to her hold a special irony.[47]

The dating of the poem is difficult to establish. We know that it was in circulation well before its appearance on the 1777 *Index*. The editor of 1898 (Cotarelo?) claims to have heard a friend of his mention having seen a manuscript dated in 1772. We know that Dorisa left Madrid in 1771 due to an illness and due also to her grief at the death of her friend María Ignacia Ibáñez. Filis's death and Dorisa's departure ended the close relationship shared among the four, Francisca, María, Nicolás, and José. Finally, death caught up with Dorisa in Valencia on April 11, 1772. The absence of elegiac sentiment or gloomy remembrances of Dorisa in the *Whores' Art* suggests that she was still very much alive when Moratín composed the poem, probably before April 1772, and most likely before Filis's death in April 1771. One month before that Moratín had written the lines quoted above: "Today I shall honor / My sweet poet's day. . . ."

In the *Whores' Art* Moratín clings close to the Spanish tradition. Erotic literature was of course a fact of literary life, even in the circumspect Spanish eighteenth century. Outside Spain it flourished openly and those who read and wrote works such as *Pamela, Moll*

Flanders, Fanny Hill, Roderick Random, Tom Jones, and *Tristam
Shandy* could rely on a Classical tradition of eroticism based on
Catullus, Petronius *(The Satyricon),* Apuleius *(The Golden Ass),*
and Ovid, to say nothing of later examples like the *Decameron,* the
Canterbury Tales, Casanova's exploits, or those of the athletic
Marquis de Sade. Spain was not so bold in the 1770s. Its social cli-
mate prohibited such works from receiving widespread attention.
But Moratín's work of "shadow literature" took little from foreign
sources and concentrated on the literature of Spain. To be sure, he
pays homage to the fictional and nonfictional likes of Diogenes,
Darius, Alexander the Great, Cesar, Homer, Virgil, Diana,
Adonis, Apollo, Bacchus, and, quite naturally, Venus. We tend to
think of his poem in terms of Ovid's *Ars amatoria,*[58] or the misogynistic tenor of Juvenal's Sixth Satire, or the openly sensual
poems of Catullus (although Moratín was uncompromisingly heter-
osexual), yet Moratín's profoundly nationalistic roots reveal themselves once more in this work. The man who had recommended the
study of "Greeks and Spaniards, Latins and Spaniards, Italians
and Spaniards, French and Spaniards, English and Spaniards" put
his theory into practice to produce a poem at once scandalous and
deeply Spanish.

The theme of syphilis, apart from revealing a personal side of the
author, is central to the poem, and it has been a literary theme since
the disease's appearance in Spain around 1500. What the Spaniards
called the "Gallic evil" (and, vindictively, the French referred to as
the "Spanish fire") began to appear as a poetic motif in Renaissance *cancioneros;* Sebastián de Horozco's *Cancionero* contains a
humorous treatment of the plight of the syphilitic.[49] Francisco
Delicado, who likewise suffered from it, so abhorred syphilis that he
produced a treatise, *El modo de adoperare el legno de India occi-
dentale* (On the Uses of the West Indies' Wood)[50], deploring the
scourges of it. Moratín claims to wish to rid the world of it, a claim
which he doubtless felt wholeheartedly. Note, though, that he does
not wish to rid the world, or even Madrid, of the carriers of it, i.e.,
the loose women who are the subjects of this poem. Hence his
counsel to a young man is that he protect himself from direct contact with the disease, and he provides a "historical" account of the
invention, by an ingenious and desperate priest, no less, of the pro-
phylactic. The description is repugnant, shockingly forthright, and
riotously nonscientific, brimming, as is the entire poem, with puns
and comic allusions:

«Si son las bubas multitud viviente
de insectos minutísimos y tiernos
como se sienten los físicos modernos,
porque el mercurio a todo bicho mata,
la comunicación evitar quiero,
haciendo escudo de la ropa santa,»
dijo, y calando a modo de sombrero
en su bendito miembro la capilla
así lo mete, la pobreta chilla,
no enseñada a tan rígida aspereza.
Acabó el fraile y ve que se endereza
la comunidad toda hacia aquel puesto
y por no dar ejemplo de inmodesto
se pone la capilla que chorrea
jabonando el cerquillo y la corona
blanco engrudo, simiente de persona. (118-19)

("If tumors are a living multitude
of very tiny and tender insects
as feel some modern scientists,
since mercury whatever bug will kill,
to avoid contact is what I will,
protecting myself with holy garb,"
he said, and like a hat he placed
upon his blessed member his cowl
and shoved it in (the girl does howl,
unused to such rigid roughness).
The friar finished and sees that toward
him the entire community begins to amble
and not wanting to set a bad example,
flips up the hood which oozes forth
upon his pate and crowns its deed
with white goo, with human seed.)

This comic scene has literary precedents. It is an ingenious parody of one of the most famous episodes in *Don Quijote* (Part 2, Chapter 17), where Sancho Panza puts some curds and whey in Don Quijote's helmet, who then proceeds unwittingly to place it on his head, and seeing them drip down, believes that his brains are leaking out. The parody is intentional, for Moratín immediately recounts: "So Don Quijote upon occasion / against his skull let loose the whey / that Sancho placed in his helmet that day." Cervantes is never far from Moratín's mind, and allusions to him and his works crop up again (114,184). One such account follows a discussion of the similarity of the technique of bullfighting (as we have seen, one of Moratín's favorite sports) with that of lovemaking (apparently another of those favorite sports), when, after numerous references which later reappear in the "Historical Letter" on bullfighting, Moratín plaintively recounts an unfortunate meeting with a rather scruffy lady of the evening: "And, thus, oh memory! Thus did I fall, / I became a fan of that false girl / whose name I do not wish to recall" ("de cuyo nombre no quiero acordarme," the famous phrase from the first paragraph of *Don Quijote* [149]).

Other literary sources or similarities are evident. Moratín's descriptions of the whores of Madrid remind us of Juan Ruiz's descriptions of the Archpriest's women (Sancha did not publish the poem until 1790; was the manuscript known in literary circles before that date?), and the couplings of his seekers of "loco amor" are gleefully described in frank terms. With equally ribald joviality Moratín presents the well-endowed La Romana (125), the "uneven" Benita (144), the "deep" Pepa la Larga (143), Beatriz, whose breasts were like two "tiny earthen jars from Toboso" (another reference to *Don Quijote,* 144), and disease-ridden Belica. In all he presents over ninety prostitutes located in over thirty sites in Madrid. Goya observed the same people and places, and, like Moratín, he turned life into art.

Not surprisingly, the greatest madame of them all, Celestina, makes an appearance. First she is introduced as a type, the lusty go-between who functioned still in the underworld of Spanish eroticism. Her eighteenth-century counterpart confides in Moratín, revealing the far-reaching effects of her considerable skills, skills which serve everyone, from grandee to beggar, nun to priest, real to "reconstructed" virgin. Then, as he had done before, Moratín confirms the literary association which the knowledgeable reader has already made by writing "Celestina was just a babe at breast, / but me, I know enough potions and tricks / for over a hundred different tasks to fix"(158).

Moratín is a superb portrait-maker who cleverly reveals the truth about a socioeconomic reality. He discusses the patronizing of prostitutes from only one point of view: the joy of sex. He has little regard for the economic implications of a society which encourages or forces women into the trade, and he shuns viewing prostitution as anything but a favorable, if somewhat risky, activity. He celebrates the uncomplicated sensuality of lovemaking without the bother of wooing, courting, or careful seductions. It is Lockeian sensualism condensed to its fundamental characteristic and without any empirical foundation. It is the discovery of the (under)world through the senses. Moratín was enlightened, but hardly liberated, and the Epicurean delight so evident in his earlier anacreontic poetry has transformed itself in the *Whores' Art* into frankly Dionysian debauchery.

Moratín sampled, directly or indirectly, the fruits of his literary heritage: Juan Ruiz, Fernando de Rojas, the Renaissance *cancioneros,* Hurtado de Mendoza, Ruíz de Alarcón, and Cervantes, among others. The fifteenth-century *Carajicomedia* has been mentioned as a forerunner of Moratín's piece in that it is also a guide to whoring spots in Madrid.[51] Likewise in his poem are traces of Quevedo's *Sueños* (Dreams) and of Diego de Torres Villarroel's *Visiones* (Visions); which both cover some of the same geographical terrain as the *Whores' Art.* Tomás de Iriarte and Felix Samaniego likewise produced pornographic literature which circulated under cover in Moratín's day. The startling aspect of Moratín's poem is the hypocrisy of it all: after all, it was he who had so vociferously objected to the immorality of the *autos* and of some Spanish Golden-Age plays. In his second Satire he had protested, "They applaud dissolute plays, / Which take pains to approve of vice, / And make the bold life agreeable" (BAE, 32), while at the same time claiming to abide by the laws of the Church (see his prologue to *Lucretia).* Here he reveals his attitude toward the power of theater in general: theater was to instruct, and as a "school for customs" it had to conform to very carefully controlled moral codes. Not so poetry. Not so, certainly then, life itself. The eighteenth-century's belief in the strength of literature, and in Moratín's case in the strength of Spanish literature, is impressively underscored.

V *Another Hero Still: Moratín Applauds Cortés*

When the Spanish Royal Academy, of which Nicolás was not a member, announced a public poetry competition in September 1777, Moratín tried his hand and presented a composition entitled "Las naves de Cortés destruidas" (Cortés's Ships Destroyed). The theme appealed to him. It was to be a poem concerning a heroic chapter of the Spanish past. Nationalistic themes had long been his favorites, and he was well qualified to enter: as the professor of poetics at the Imperial College, he was respected in Madrid for the seriousness with which he approached literature, and he had friends in high places, both literary and political. Above all, he was an outstanding poet. The academy's deadline for entries was March 31, 1778, which Moratín, whose speed writing is well known to us, easily met. Forty-five poems were entered, among them a short one by the Salamancan School poet José Iglesias de la Casa, in which he praised Flumisbo and Dalmiro. Moratín expected to win, but the academy disappointed those expectations, for on August 13, 1778, it awarded the prize to an unknown younger poet, José María Vaca de Guzmán, even though not everyone considered Nicolás's to be inferior.[52] Leandro, chafed by the academy's snub, later attempted to convince the public that Nicolás had never entered the competition. Facts prove him wrong. The very manuscript is still kept at the academy, and the last page clearly states that it was officially entered on March 17, 1778, and seen by members Francisco Capilla, Antonio Murillo, Vicente de la Huerta, Tomás Sánchez, José Guevara, Manuel Uriarte, Felipe Samaniego, Juan de Aravaca, Gaspar de Montoya, Fernando Màgallón, Enrique Ramos, the Duke of Villahermosa, Benito Bails, and José Vela.

Nicolás died before the poem was published, which Leandro undertook as a homage of respect to his father. But when it came out in 1785 it was in a form different from that which we know to be the original,[53] and to it were added a prologue and some interesting "Critical Reflections." John Dowling's recent work has at last enabled us to put the polemic over "Cortés's Ships" into perspective.[54] Once again, it is a question of real authorship of the best-known version, whether it is purely Nicolás's or whether Leandro "improved" it. The most accessible and widely known version is that which appeared in the BAE, but it is not faithful to the original manuscript. There are three extant versions: 1) the original manuscript of 1778, only recently published (is it Moratín's or was it written by a scribe?), 2) the version brought out in 1785 by Leandro,[55] which contains revisions and omissions (122 strophes reduced to 104); and 3) a version reduced by nearly half (to sixty-five strophes) and published again by Leandro in the 1821 *PW*. Quintana reproduced the 1785 version in his *Select Castilian Poetry* in 1807, 1817, and again in 1830, and in 1846, when the BAE undertook the publication of the complete works of Moratín the Elder, this same version was chosen as being the most complete. Cayetano Rosell published the truncated 1821 version in his own BAE 29 on epic poetry. The real mystery is why the manuscript, which the Royal Academy has possessed and even displayed for public viewing, remained unpublished for 200 years.

As was the case with the "Bullfight Festival in Madrid," Nicolás's production is more varied, longer, and richer in detail than the shortened version that is generally known to the public. Even fifty years after his death there were "few who do not know this epic poem,"[56] attesting to its attractions. Written in royal octaves (strophes of eight hendecasyllabic verses with a consonantal rhyme pattern of ABABABCC) as was standard for heroic cantos, the poem's structure is somewhat similar to that of the "Bullfight Festivals." The author's prologue comprises the first three strophes, in which he states his purpose: "I shall sing the courage of the Hispanic Captain / . . . / If it is suited for verse and if Apollo inspires me." The long core of the poem comes to our attention as clamorous noises introduce the arrival of troops (4), who are described by name in colorful detail. The soldiers receive respectful treatment from Moratín; he carefully enumerates their physical attributes, associating each with past deeds or armaments suggesting valor, courage, and strength (5-21). The Indian maiden Marina comes into focus in a lively description; we are touched by her beauty and entranced with the possibility of the love theme which will complicate Cortés's activities in the New World (22-25). She speaks, anxious to hear details of the soldiers before her (26); Aguilar, Cortés's main lieutenant, answers her, and the catalogue of participants continues (27-40). They come from all over Spain. It is indeed a national army, encompassing all the geographical points of the peninsula, underscoring the patriotic nature of Cortés's endeavor. Moratín emphasizes this in order to impart a broad nationalistic tone to the poem. It is more than the glorification of one man, it is the glorification of a whole country, and each reader surely would identify with the soldier who represented his own local region.

A young soldier, page to Cortés, appears breathless with the news of the captain's imminent arrival (41). The first climax begins to build with noise and jubilation (42). The crescendo of excitement explodes as Cortés makes his entrance. The exclamations that were to subvert Moratín's intentions in *Hormesinda* are quite effective here; we are dazzled by Cortés's finery, his steed, his commanding presence (43-50):

Cortés, el gran Cortés: Divina Clio,
Tu alto influxo mi espíritu levante;
¿Quién jamás hubo objeto como el mío,
Ni tan glorioso Capitán triunfante?
¡Con qué aspeto real, y señorío
Se le muestra a su exército delante!
¡O qué valor que obstenta! ¡y qué nobleza!
¡O quánta heroycidad y gentileza! (43)

(Cortés, the great Cortés: Clio divine,
  Let lift my spirit your noble bent:
  Who ever had an object such as mine,
  Or so glorious a Captain in triumph sent?
  With what grace and royal visage shine
  Before his army then he went!
  What valor! And what nobility!
  Oh, so much courage and such gentility!)

He views his troops and fires them up in a stirring speech (51-58),
but dissent is in the ranks: several soldiers have grave doubts about
the approaching tasks and discussions ensue. Cortés attempts to
convince them of the integrity of his calling (59-72), but devilish
forces intervene to cause trouble (73-83). Only death awaits, they
fear:

No de otra suerte, o con menor estruendo
Desgajándose el polo centellante,
Sangriento el Sol y Luna obscureciendo,
Rebentando el Ynfierno horror tronante:
Los astros de sus círculos cayendo
Naturaleza absorta, y titubeante,
Temblarán Cielo, tierra y Mar profundo
En la profetizada fin del Mundo. (84)

(No other way, or with less sound
  The pole splits off, brightly gleaming,
  The darkened moon, the bloodied sun,
  And Hell explodes in horror streaming:
  Stars from their bands are coming down,
  Entranced is nature, unstable being,
  Heaven, earth, and deep sea — the World —
  Shall quake; its end has been foretold.)

The soldiers' fears and doubts increase. They grumble at their
fate, questioning the sense of the proposed campaign and con-

vinced that if the inclement weather or the menace of nature do not defeat them, then they will be eaten by savages at Montezuma's command. Their gloom paralyzes them (85-97) and rebellion is considered (98). In another stirring speech, Cortés attempts to assure them of success and to promise them fame for their efforts (98-102). He plays upon their patriotism and their proven heroic nature; Moratín's superb listing of their merits is indeed inspiring. The use of dialogue again heightens the dramatic impact, and the shifts in point of view add diversity and interest. Still, the soldiers refuse (103) and Cortés's only recourse is the act that inspired the poem — the torching of the ships, the soldiers' only means of escape. The scenes of the burning of the ships (104-16) are marvelous, informed by rapid action and brilliant description. They build slowly, as do the flames, and engulf the reader in the desperate and heroic act. The deed is done (117) when from the sky there descends a dove, flying toward Mexico in a touchingly symbolic prefiguration of the Spaniards' future course (118). The troops are inspired (119-20). The poet has done his job (121-22).

He has also modified history. Dowling has shown how Moratín expanded upon his sources, significantly, by inventing the burning-of-the-ships episode. Contemporary documents and historians provide no evidence that Cortés actually set fire to the ships, suggesting instead that he destroyed them by running them aground. Even the academy directed only that the poem should deal with the "destruction" of Cortés's ships, or how Cortés "sinks"[57] the vessels. Moratín's work was the first to contain this episode and to enjoy wide diffusion. That later authors and historians began to accept as "fact" the burning of the ships attests to the impact of Moratín's poem on the consciousness of the nineteenth and twentieth centuries. Moratín was a poet, not a historian, and he permitted his poetic imagination a degree of latitude that more careful authors would have avoided. He was capable of anachronism (as in the "Bullfight Festival") and pure invention (the Cid as bullfighter, the burning of these ships) for dramatic impact. Such inventions heightened the narrative interest of the poems, sharpened the details of the presentation, and allowed Moratín to focus on a climax. Certainly it lacked verisimilitude, but that, apparently, was something that only dramatists, not Moratín as a poet, had to worry about. Was he aware of these transpositions and additions? It is easy to think that he was not; he wrote quickly and not particularly carefully. He frequently jumbled his facts. On the other hand, he had friends who were historians and who may have informed him of inaccuracies in detail, but which he chose to include anyway for their literary effects. Certainly Signorelli, who read the poem in 1777,[58] offered no modifications that we know of.

The form of Moratín's poem is Classical — Classical in the sense that the rhetorical devices are based on a tradition long recognized as suitable for epic poetry (models such as Horace, Cicero, Quintillian, and Aristotle) and enthusiastically incorporated by Spanish poets since the Renaissance. The content is purely Spanish, and, as we have seen right along, the division between Classical and Spanish is, in Moratín's mind, a false one. The elimination of those boundaries produces some interesting results, that we would tend not to expect from an author who years before had so vociferously argued against the unruly mixture of antagonistic elements on stage. In the poem, Moratín blithely mixes one pagan mythology (Classical) with another pagan mythology (Aztec), and then couches both in a Christian terminology. With equal ease he speaks of Apollo (1), Pyeride (2), Cupid (8), or Adonis (16) alongside Quauhtemuch (92) and Miscuac (92), then likens the entire undertaking to the Christian conquest of the Moors for the greater glory of God and country. The Christian imagery dominates, of course, but we would expect a man who was bitterly opposed to depicting Christ's crucifixion in Madrid to be more careful with his own juxtapositions. Moratín never believed in "what's good for the goose is good for the gander." He allowed himself freedoms which he denied to others.

Leandro apparently had access to a manuscript of the "Cortés's Ships" which he reworked and published, along with the aid of Juan Antonio Loche, in 1785. Loche added some interesting "Critical Reflections," reprinted later in the BAE, in which he discusses the poem's content, form, possible sources (Lope's *Jerusalén,* Canto 19, is mentioned), and literary merit. They do not add anything to our understanding or appreciation of the poem itself, but they do demonstrate the high regard which Loche had for the poem and his expectations that the public would share his opinion. The prologue to the poem is more aggressive. In it the author states categorically that Nicolás's poem was not entered in the academy's contest, for, had it been, it surely would have triumphed over the winner: "I believe with certainty that if Moratín's poem was composed then [for the contest], it was not presented for whatever reasons."[59] Such a statement is a falsehood, as the author of the prologue, be it Leandro or Loche, well knew. It did not stop him from puffing up Nicolás's image, as Leandro would do again in the admirable, but biased, *Life* he attached to the *PW* of 1821, although by that date he admitted that the poem *was* turned in to the academy. It seems certain that the author of the "Critical Reflections" was also the author of the prologue attached to the work. He writes: "Persuaded, then, that the only way to [present the poem] was to do a dispassionate examination of this Epic Canto, without getting into generalities which are of no use, I have tried to do it as best I could." Leandro may have "corrected" the poem and then let Loche present the critical commentary on it, but until further documentary evidence is produced we will not know for sure whether Loche actually wrote them or whether his petition was merely a cover for Leandro, who may have wanted to appear objectively disinterested.

Naturally, the winning poet, Vaca de Guzmán, would not let his honor and reputation stand for the slurs, opinions, and outright lies published in the "Critical Reflections," so he produced his own "Advertencias que hace . . . DJMVG, autor del canto Las Naves de Cortés destruıdas, único premiado y publicado por la Real Academia Española . . . "[60] (Remarks by DJMVG, Author of Cortés's Ships Destroyed, the Only Poem Cited and Published by the Spanish Royal Academy . . .) two years later. Vaca conceded that don Nicolás was a "poet of known merit," but that his poem was so inferior it did not even receive the academy's support for publication, while he cast aside all suggestions that the poem was not placed in competition. The "Remarks," written in a tone of (false) modesty and reaching for sympathy in a "poor-unknown-me" way, are devastating. The battle became one of the unknown young poet/David against the mature, established professor/Goliath and the results are, he argues, public knowledge. He enumerates Moratín's poem's failings, and significantly many of the words and verses he attacks as frail or inappropriate are precisely those changed by 1821. Moreover, he knew and stated publicly that Moratín's poem had been "corrected and touched up in its first printing."

The 1785 version, then, was different from the original manuscript, and the 1821 version was more different still. Dowling's statistical table reveals the number of "corrections" made:

Version	Strophes	Verses	Strophes Eliminated	Verses Changed
holograph	122	976	—	—
1785	104	832	18	74
1821	65	520	39	264[61]

From 1778 to 1785 the following strophes disappeared entirely: 11 (description of Ruano and Olid and their steeds), 15 (Escalante, "the horror of Moors," brave bullfighter and Mexia), 18-20 (bright description of clothing and jewelry; Orozco, Vaena, Guzmán, Roxas number among the able troops), 24 (a delicate portrait of Marina in a mixture of Christian and Aztec finery), 27 (Aguilar describes some of the men for Marina), 33-37 (more individuals, presented by name, place, and outstanding characteristic), 40 (a priest is introduced), 80-81 (prediction of the glorious reign of Carlos III), 109-11 (the lively description of the ships sinking slowly into the water). Strophes 28-30 are transposed in the 1785 version, appearing in reverse order. In addition to eliminating complete strophes, the editor of 1785 revised syllable count in numerous verses. Many examples of this abound, yet by 1821 Leandro was not satisfied with these changes, and he rewrote nearly the entire poem. As we saw above, the length is reduced by almost half, and the other emendations are so pervasive that the poem ceases to belong to Nicolás. It is only in Leandro's maturity that he cast aside his father's listing of the soldiers serving Cortés, for when he handed in his own "A la toma de Granada" (The Siege of Granada) for the academy's 1779 convocation he consciously imitated this very same stylistic technique.

Quantitatively Moratín's original is richer than that which appeared in the *PW*, but the important aspect is that it is qualitatively richer as well. As he did with the "Bullfight Festival," Leandro rejected his father's interest in the details of the story. The proper names, the descriptions of arms, dress, and manners, and many of the individuals who personalize the poem disappear. Nicolás's poem is warmer, more vibrant, and more exciting. The direct intervention of the author lends an unexpected intimacy to the poem, and the use of dialogue intensifies its dramatic nature. It possesses a grandeur and a scope curtailed by Leandro's more severe idea of what epic poetry should be. The "superfluous" details are gone, but except for minor lexical changes and the obviously anachronistic references to Carlos III's reign, Leandro's changes do little to improve his father's original conception of Cortés's heroic action. After all, Nicolás had warned us as early as 1763 that "a grand and heroic matter / cannot be whispered about."[62]

VI *Miscellaneous Poetry*

Moratín published several poems independently of the *Poet*. While they are not his best poems they are important ones since they were among those which reached a wider public. We need to keep in mind that the *Poet* contained a limited number of poems, and that the majority of his poetical works appeared only after his death.

A. *In Praise of Carlos III*

As Moratín was waiting for the chance to express his enthusiasm for the new king, Carlos III, the opportunity presented itself when Carlos pardoned several condemned criminals on September 20, 1762.[63] Moratín, the queen's "servant," and already a member of the poetic club called the Arcadians of Rome, completed a four-page, 163-verse poem praising the event of the king's magnaminity. Two characteristics distinguish it from the poems he would collect and publish in a couple of years: it lacks his usual avalanche of historical, mythological, and literary references, and it is infused with a series of religious associations normally absent from his poetry. It does, though, contain a prosiness and a recourse to exclamation ("Oh, august Carlos! / Oh, pious one! Oh, father of the nation! Oh, just one!") that at times infuse his later verse and much of his theater. We have no information about the poem's reception.

B. *Flumisbo, Shepherd-Warrior*

Moratín's first lengthy poetical work to appear in print was a poem he wrote in response to a celebration carried out in the Royal Academy of San Fernando in 1763. The academy had commissioned works in praise of Luis de Velasco and Vicente González, Spanish war heroes who had died in the defense of the Morro castle in Havana, Cuba, when it was besieged by the British in the summer of 1762. The loss of Cuba was an ignominious defeat and a severe blow to Spanish strength in Latin America, but nevertheless González and Velasco were lauded as heroes, and portraits of the two were presented to the academy; Moratín's "Eclogue to Velasco and González" was completed by mid-July 1763.[64]

The eclogue form, the initial pastoral content, and the two interlocutors, the shepherds Coridon and Lucindo, are very reminiscent of the poetry of Garcilaso, whom Moratín deeply admired and was even to "steal from" later. In this dialogue between Coridon and Lucindo, the latter represents a faintly veiled emotional persona of Nicolás, who reveals his feelings and political allegiances. Lucindo, "in Mantua born," guards the "flocks" of Carlos III, the king called to rule by Isabel. Lucindo has just returned from a visit to the court and he details his response to the awesome capital, where art imitates nature's grandeur and even outshines it in splendor and opulence. He talks of the paintings and sculptures he has enjoyed, and of the grand scale of Madrid's official buildings. These emotions were no doubt echoes of Nicholás's honest response to Madrid when he returned to it in late 1759. It was breathtakingly exciting and splendid; this attitude remained with him throughout his career.

The core of the poem abandons pastoral themes for epic ones, for it is Lucindo's recounting of the deeds of the two heroes in terms that are reminiscent of Moratín's later handling of similar concerns. When Coridon questions the validity of praising warlike things, Lucindo defends the need to sing of heroic deeds, and Lucindo's response is Moratín's himself, who some years later returned to Spanish heroes to write both the play *Guzmán el Bueno* (1777) and the epic poem "Cortés's Ships Destroyed" (1778). His description of Velasco is an inspiring and idealized portrait of a hero, similar to the one he would use again when describing Cortés, and the following patriotic sentiments are similar to those he will develop in *Guzmán.*

> Veréis rendir primero
> Mi vida que mi espada;
> Mi rey, mi religión, mi patria amada
> Verán que soy cristiano y caballero,
> Y todo el mundo entero
> No bastará a rendir a mis soldados,
> Curtidos a los hielos y a los soles,
> Pocos, pero arrestados,
> Y todos verdaderos españoles. (BAE, 23)
>
> (I would give up

My life before my sword;
My king, religion and beloved country
Will see that I am a gentleman and a Christian.
And the entire world
Will not suffice to overcome my troops
Hardened to ice and to sun,
Few but daring,
And all true Spaniards.)

The unexpected juxtaposition of the pastoral form with the epic content produces a dislocation in the reader. Moratín seems unable to define his poetic voice here, and while intellectually attracted to the shepherd's mode, his emotional outpourings pull him toward the nationalistic breast-beating that would become so characteristic of his writings. The imagery and the points of reference are not those of the traditional eclogue, but rather those of more martial verse. The poem is a change in the conventional shepherd-tells-a-shepherd's-story (usually based on unrequited or lost love): it is a shepherd-tells-a-soldier's-story. The outer shell of Moratín's poem is pastoral, but the core is epic. The almost perfect balance in the poem's structure points to this. The 362 verses can be divided into three parts: the first part is a pastoral introduction and dialogue of forty-five verses; the second is the poem's center, Lucindo's account of Madrid, the heroes, and most of all their military achievements, recounted in 268 verses; and the third is another forty-nine-verse dialogue between the two shepherds, discussing briefly the merits of dealing with war themes. The first and third parts serve as a parenthesis to the central action. This poem previews the major concerns which would become evident the following year when the *Poet* began to appear in Madrid bookshops, for in that periodical's first poem he states clearly that " . . . my numerous verses shall praise / The country and her most famous sons" *(Poet,* 1, BAE, 19).

C. *A Poetic Grab-Bag:* Diana o el arte de la caza

Moratín's life was integrally involved with those of the royal family. He grew up with them at La Granja; he played with the princes, entertained the queen with his early poems, moved to Madrid with Carlos III, and suffered the death of his Isabel. His poems abound in sincere respect for Carlos, love for Isabel, and friendship for younger royal family members. The abundance of his favorable remarks regarding the royal family indicates a sincere belief in their worth, not a superficial or sycophantic collection of positive references to them. His respect was genuine, not just dutiful.

Moratín's longest poem (2,628 verses) is directed to Luis Antonio Jaime, son of Felipe V and Isabel de Farnesio, the younger brother of Carlos III. Luis was ten years older than Nicolás, thirty-eight at the time Nicolás directed this poem to him in 1765, yet to Moratín they were almost "brothers" (strophe 5). *Diana o el arte de la caza* (Diana or the Art of the Hunt)[65] is a conglomeration of history, philosophy, encomium, reminiscence, and harangue which Moratín wrote on the occasion of Luis's approaching betrothal. It ostensibly belongs to the long tradition of the *De regimine principum,* for in it Moratín sets out to discuss the origins, development, and present state of Luis's favorite sport, the hunt, and to instruct him in its prudent execution.

To ward off criticism that he was convinced would be leveled at him, he included a twelve-page prologue to the published version of the poem. It is a seemingly surprising document coming from him, for in it he protests that "it is impossible to observe all the rules that they prescribe . . . and besides there are no works that observe them [all]." Moratín against the rules? No; his position is consistent with his previously declared use of the rules as guides or aides to good art, to "good taste." But he had been (and is) criticized for a fanatical attachment to all the rules in all cases which is, of course, absurd, so he defended himself *a priori.* He also defends the "usefulness" of his poem and the value of treating scientific matters in verse — a particularly Neoclassical stance — as well as his use of what has been derided as pedantry since, as he sees it, "the poet is not to blame for the ignorance of his readers." Such comments could not have endeared him to the reading public, whose tastes he was so strenuously trying to reform.

He divides his didactic poem into six cantos: I, the origins of the hunt; II, its dangers and the equipment the hunter needs; III, the importance of horses and of, curiously, astrology; IV, the hunting of fowl; V, the hunting of wild animals; and VI, a description of a hunt. But he is easily sidetracked from his main theme, and included in the poem are myriad extraneous tidbits of opinion or information that distract the reader (and presumably Luis, the listener) from the central purpose. On the topic he displays a knowledge of his subject, possibly learned from his youthful days at La

Granja, and he is able to present in admirable detail a catalogue of the birds, beasts, and armaments generally associated with the hunt. It is crammed with information and ideas, mythological personages, contemporary science, drama, and visual imagery. Even Garcilaso and Dorisa make appearances. Yet little is worth remembering as poetry or even as an encyclopedia of facts. It is complete, but frequently patronizing, as if he were addressing an absolutely knowledgeless individual. Much of it is muddled or pseudoscientific; and it is plagued with digressions; Moratín tends to veer wildly off track, abruptly changing moods, frame of reference, and even to whom he addresses the work (the "you" of the poem fluctuates without warning, encompassing Diana, Luis, God, the muses, and even various animals and birds). The avalanche of Classical and historical allusions becomes tedious, and the standardization of the metric pattern is numbing: 2,628 verses of hendecasyllabic sextets in invariable ABABCC consonantal rhyme. In its time it was rated "one of the best didactic poems to be published in Spain,"[66] but Leandro included only selections of it in the 1821 *PW*.

Still, some interesting thoughts are expressed in the poem, and Moratín has his successful moments. Like the *Whores' Art,* it instructs a young man in an art, and like the *Whores' Art* it contains a catalogue (of birds and animals vs. loose women) of their associative characteristics. Names are brought forth from personality traits, famous deeds, or places of origin (a device he used again in "Cortés's Ships"). As we have seen before and shall see again, Moratín is caught up in the excitement of battle, and some of the poem's moments of heightened tension come when he is describing the visual and auditory effects of war. He has done this from the "Eclogue to Velasco and González" through his plays and up to "Cortés's Ships," negating his early disclaimer that epic themes and the concerns of Mars were not for him; as we have clearly seen, they were. His thesis here is that the hunt *is* war, and while he fails to sustain the image throughout the poem, he offers curious examples of the link between the two: man, not content with hunting animals, turns to hunting other men; the hunter and the soldier have much in common; as a good lieutenant knows his enemy's field positions, so does the hunter; Fernán González, Alexander the Great, and others learned their skills from the hunt; the hunt is not a reflection of war, but rather war is an image of the hunt; and so on. Political overtones emerge, and the false foreign customs which

Moratín satirized in *La petimetra* appear again when he claims, "Nor have native customs been corrupted / By foreign ones" (strophe 70).

The "philosophy" of the *Diana* ranges from Renaissance and Golden Age, learned no doubt from his readings of Lope and Calderón, but hardly attributed to them ("And we should not act with passion, / Since extremes are always vices," strophe 84), to the enlightened (praise for modern scientists such as Bacon, Locke, Leibniz, Newton, and the "solid ideas" of "Feijoo, my great Feijoo," strophe 434), to folklore, old wives' tales, and conventional wisdom. He integrates many of the accepted ideas of the above-mentioned men of science, and he demonstrates an attraction toward "reason," but his faith in experimental science has well-defined restrictions, and it comes to a full stop when any "barbarous atheist" (strophe 168) negates the presence of "God, whom I adore," or who "denies that there is a master" (strophe 169), because he fails to comprehend His essence. So Locke and Newton have value only insofar as they fit into the prearranged and God-centered cosmology. Moratín fits into his times, and we see him as enlightened in certain respects, but only as a product of a Spanish Enlightenment, restricted, like "Spanish Naturalism," to those views that do not threaten the established world-view. Still, he does attack pseudoscience, and it is not difficult to read a severe reproach of the likes of Torres Villarroel (still alive in 1765) in the warning: "Do not imitate the shallowness / Of fanatical prophetic astrologers / Who over man's free choice and will / Wish to place strict conditions" (strophe 174). This vacillation between a seemingly modern approach to the world around him and a placid acceptance of outmoded ideas reveals the ambiguity of Moratín's personality, that conflict in him which manifests itself on so many levels. He fights what he views to be a new-wave battle against shoddy dramaturgy, careless lyricism, and the forces of ignorance, but in part it is a rear-guard action against the slipping away of traditional values, both literary and social. *Diana* captures the shifting nature of his thinking, and the result — in various degrees entertaining, autobiographical, contradictory, boring, sincere, knowledgeable, and stimulating — sums up his entire literary career.

D. *"The Singer of the Maidens"*

The three poems that Moratín composed and read aloud at the

annual prize ceremonies for the Royal Economic Society in 1777, 1778, and 1779 earned him the nickname of "El cantor de las doncellas" (he says in the 1779 poem, " . . . I am in Maredit named / The honest singer of the maidens"). They also earned him the derision of his friend, Tomás de Iriarte, who could not resist the temptation to satirize what he saw as Nicolás's fatuous hyperbole and hollow flattery of the society's activities. Each of the poems was published separately,[67] subsidized by the Archbishop of Toledo, who each year was in attendance and who supported the society's functions. Of the three, only the first (1777) and the third (1779) reappear in the BAE (7-8 and 27-31), and the reprinted version of the 1777 poem differs from that which was published in the *Memoirs* of the Economic Society. Since it was included in the *PW* (105-11), the changes were most likely effected by Leandro, and once again Nicolás's leisurely pace and attention to detail are severely clipped back (419 verses in the original; only 148 in that published by Leandro) .

Moratín stood before those attending the first prize ceremonies of the society on Wednesday, December 24, 1777, and read a ballad praising the industry of the young girls who worked and studied at the society's schools. We saw that Moratín was interested early on in the goals of the Royal Economic Society, and how he attempted, with limited success, to contribute to the technical concerns of the group. But his talents lay less with treatises on agricultural production or weaving technique than with the aesthetic side of those endeavors. He became the poetic cheerleader for the society, and was, until his death, that corporation's unofficial poetic spokesman. He was composing the "Cortés's Ships" for that other academy at the same time he was delivering this verse statement, yet here he once again eschews the warlike themes which were so dominant in his art *(Guzmán el Bueno* had just recently appeared): "I have no wish to sing / Of military manners / Of armaments and heroes, / Or standards or of banners." Rather, he will praise the "chorus of maidens" whose "helpful hands" and "tireless zeal" have brought them all together for congratulations. As a good enlightened thinker, Moratín praises work (in a most un-Epicurean way he refers to "perfidious Cupid" and "disgraceful dance"). He seems to be sincerely impressed with what so many of his countrymen have achieved under the knowledgeable rule of Carlos III, as much men in battle as these girls on other fronts, particularly in the weaving trades. His idealized picture of these "busy bees," spin-

ning merrily and accompanying their work with songs, is hardly
representative of the facts of their working existence. Their work
and working conditions were far from the blissful setting that
Moratín describes, which he of course knew. It was his art that
demanded, on these occasions, such selectivity to portray a
pleasant, positive impression.

Moratín painted a lovely scene with sufficient verbal color to
praise and flatter the industriousness of the girls selected to win
that year's prizes. He was impressed that they did not fret away
their time "moving / Their bodies in crude dance," but rather applied their energies to work "without wasting an instant." That
work ethic and Moratín's respect for it dominate the tone of all
three of the poems; work was something he believed in. Even while
he pretended to play and to enjoy the hedonistic life or when he was
not gainfully employed (as jewelkeeper, lawyer, professor, or government censor) he nevertheless worked — at his art. The girls'
work, virtue, industry, and motivation become important to
Moratín as an indication of both the past under Carlos III and the
future of his country. Flattery will get him anywhere, so he was in-
vited back year after year to sing the praises of the society and of
the girls working in its trade schools.

The 1777 poem received a polite reception at its reading and a
generally widespread applause upon its publication. But with one
individual its reception was far from positive. Tomás de Iriarte
used it as the basis for a satirical jab at his friend Moratín. His
"Vejamen" (Lampoon), larded with biting humor, attacks
Moratín's participation in the Royal Economic Society and particularly his overblown verse in praise of the "girls." Iriarte riotously
and rightly accuses the Economic Society of "economizing" on the
prizes — fifteen *reales* per winner (some of the prizes were somewhat more generous) hardly were the "treasure" or "golden coins"
mentioned by Moratín the following year. Moratín, who sang the
praises of Hormesinda and Guzmán and who wrote an *Art* "similar
to Ovid's," comes under Iriarte's attack by referring to the school's
students as "young girls" when, in fact, one was twenty-six, one
thirty-three, and two were forty years old! "Notice to the Public:"
writes Iriarte, "any woman wishing to shed the weight of years
should work in the Royal Economic Society schools, and she will
hear herself always called 'little girl.'" The poem also mocks
Moratín's reading voice ("an ever-lasting sing-song"), his writing
style (a use of alliterative 'p' sounds at the poem's beginning, the

tautological phrasing), and even his judgment (Iriarte categorically refuses to consider the girls "young," "beautiful," "chaste," "pure," "clean," or "virginal"). He accuses Moratín of making them sound like novice nuns, suggesting that this new emphasis on chastity is Moratín's repentance for having written his outrageous *Whores' Art;* some model he is for the boys at the Imperial College, Iriarte writes. He even, in a most un-Neoclassical manner, pronounces Moratín's verses "cold."

Moratín countered with a "friendly reproach" to Iriarte[68] in which he defended his own easy-flowing verse and his simplicity and revealed that he was offended and hurt by Iriarte's frivolous attack. Iriarte's comments are "unworthy" of him and they are unjust payment for a good friendship, as well as insulting to the archbishop and to the society itself. Moratín felt very protective of the society's goals, its good works, and its enlightened stance, and he was chastened by attempts to denigrate them, to say nothing of his dislike for personal criticism. Surprisingly, though, their friendship was not damaged by Iriarte's jabs. When Iriarte wrote *Donde las dan las toman* (Give and Take), a burlesque commentary on López Sedano's *Parnaso Español,* Moratín supported it with his own verse letter in sixty-six tercets which he sent to Iriarte. The latter responded again with a ballad (BAE, v. 63, 62–63) and sent it to Nicolás with a cover letter attesting to their "sincere friendship."[69] In the poem Iriarte confesses to having thought Moratín "gentle," "innocent," and "compassionate," but this latter's attack on Sedano was apparently such that Iriarte now considered Moratín to be "intrepid," "crude," and "rigorous." No matter. This was all merely literary play and Moratín refused to take Iriarte's comments with undue seriousness in the final analysis.

In 1778 Moratín's creation was an "Eclogue, Dorisa and Amarilis," which was less of a dialogue than a monologue by Dorisa, encouraged at intervals by the other shepherdess. Dorisa describes her experience of going to Madrid (it sounds very like the first eclogue he published in 1763) to collect one of the society's prizes. It is an idealized description of the charm of enlightened Madrid, protected by Carlos III. Dorisa prattles on about the luxurious surroundings, the amenable work, the rich prizes to be won (!), the "paternal love" showered on the young girls by the important men of the court. It was read to the society on August 22; by October it was printed and distributed to local society members as well as sent out to regional groups in Talavera, Vergara,

Valencia, Tenerife, Zaragoza, Seville, and other places.[70]

The 1779 poem is interesting for two specific reasons: 1) it is the last poem which Moratín made public before he died in May of 1780, and 2) it contains a wealth of topographical information about Madrid. Madrid played an important role in his poetry from the very beginning (we remember Lucindo's reaction to the court; see also the "Madrid, Ancient and Modern" that was collected in the *PW*, 154-55; BAE, 38), and both the "Bullfight Festival" and the *Whores' Art* present perspectives on it. This public reading contained so many insights into historical and geographical Madrid that Moratín included some explanatory notes with it, and when the BAE published it the editors talked another of Madrid's famous supporters, Ramón de Mesonero Romanos, into expanding upon them. The result is a brief history and travelogue of the capital city written in 145 hendecasyllabic tercets. It is more ponderous than his first ballad to the society, but his wanderings through Madrid and his obvious respect for the inherent value of the detailed description of his native city prefigure that similar interest developed by the costumbrista and Realist novelists. It no doubt had high audience appeal as well, since his listeners could readily identify with his references to their own streets or to places familiar to them. Still, while being of some historical interest, its poetic value is minimal. Moratín sets up no conceptual poetic structure except the call, from all over Madrid, of the girls who attend the society's schools. There are no points of metaphorical interest and no original insights into the poetic nature of Madrid. Madrid is merely there, historical and static, but not alive. Moratín's focus is scholarly rather than poetic and the resulting poem holds interest only in the former aspect, never in the latter.

VII   *Conclusions: Poetry of Love*

Moratín's poetry is a poetry infused with love: love of women (Dorisa, Madrid's prostitutes, the girls of the Royal Economic Society, Isabel de Farnesio), love of his country, manifest in poems about Spanish heroes (Velasco and González, Cortés,) Spanish nobles (Carlos III, the Duke of Medinasidonia, Aranda, the princes), or the country's capital; love of the bullfight; and love of poetry itself. These are the four concerns around which he guided the discussions at the San Sebastián Inn. They are the ones which shine forth from his most successful poems.

He was attracted to knowledge, and the richness of the world around him elicited from him keen observations and even catalogues of the surrounding reality. His concerns were those of his day, humanistic and enlightened. In *Diana* he provides an encyclopedic catalogue of animals and birds, each with an associative characteristic, a technique which he favored as evidenced in his *Whores' Art* catalogue of ladies of the evening, the "Cortés's Ships" listing of the men involved in that perilous journey, or the Moorish soldiers and regalia in the "Bullfight Festival" and in the ballads. Even the poems to the "girls" of the Royal Economic Society receive similar stylistic treatment.

The poetry vacillates between seemingly opposing poles: the Epicurean seductiveness of women and wine ("celebrated Epicureus" was an inspiration for *Diana)* and the Good-Citizen posture evident in poems ranging from his first praises of Carlos III to his last endeavors at the Economic Society. His feelings of desire are as frequently mingled with pain and rejection as with pleasure and fulfillment. Much of what he wrote was, naturally, convention that followed the fashions of his day (literary fashions that he was instrumental in establishing). Still, the consistency with which he personalized the poems, when combined with what we understand to be his emotional and intellectual landscape, leaves little doubt that he put himself into his verses. They are not dry scribbles, and while limited in scope, they nonetheless shed important light on Moratín's sensibilities. As Glendinning suggests, Moratín almost lived his poetry.[71]

Many of the poems fail to supercede the rhetoric of the time or the artificial posture of the author. Some of the so-called enlightened poems, like others produced in the eighteenth century, are tedious. Many others, though, succeed in their grace, honesty, and enthusiasm. The best are elegant and learned, passionate and subtle. Moratín was a teacher of poetry, a talker of poetry, a critic of poetry, and above all, a poet. He was influential in raising Spanish lyric poetry to a level of concern, care, and thoughtfulness that it had not reached in nearly seventy-five years; on his examples were built the foundations of a renovation in the Spanish poetic genre, a renovation continued by the Salamancan School of poetry in which Moratín's close friend Cadalso was a participant. Cadalso even begged Moratín to send him copies of his poems so that they could be read and studied in the "Academy"[72] in Salamanca. Cadalso claimed that Meléndez Valdés and another friend clamored for Moratín's verses, "as if I carried them around in my pocket," and saw part of his own poetry being shaped, even at a distance, by Moratín: Cadalso's elegy to Filis ("Oh! rompa ya el silencio el dolor mío!" [Oh, let this pain of mine break the silence!]) was directly modeled on Flumisbo's elegy to Isabel de Farnesio. And Cadalso, by return post, used to send Meléndez's verses to Moratín to be shared with his colleagues at San Sebastián. Moratín's achievements did not catch him "unawares" or "surprise" from him fine verses;[73] while some were written perhaps too quickly, they were based on thought, years of study, and a rich enthusiasm for the craft of poetry.

His best poems capture the urgently exciting spirit of his Spain — both past and present — and bring to it a style firmly grounded in the tradition of his country's past artists. Several of them remain among the century's most respected poems. He was intensely conscious of his Spanish heritage, and while he was keenly respectful of the Classical masters — primarily Pindar, Anacreon, Horace, Homer, Ovid, and Virgil — he is a direct descendant of Garcilaso, Villegas, Herrera, Quevedo, Lope, and other Spanish Renaissance and Golden-Age poets. It was he who recommended the study of Greeks, Romans, French, Italians, etc., *and Spaniards* at each turn. The poetic works of the Spanish poets were undergoing a revival of interest in precisely the years in which Moratín was writing (and in the prologue to the *Poet* he had called for new editions of their works): López Sedano's *Parnaso Español* began to appear in 1768, Ríos published his edition of Villegas's poetry in 1774, and an edition of Garcilaso's poetry had come out nine years earlier.

Moratín's respect for Garcilaso as an inspiration and as a model ran particularly deep. He frequently included forms, tone, vocabulary, ambience, and even direct quotations from Garcilaso in his poems. When he persuaded Conti to translate the First Eclogue into Italian, the published version (1771) had appended to it four poems by Moratín celebrating the gifted poet. Only one of these was included in the *PW* or the BAE (and in a very different form; Leandro put his hand in again). Italian poetry interested him and he read and discussed it with pleasure (he even copied some of Petrarch); French poets played little part in his creative process, although he was conversant in the poetic achievements of Corneille, Racine, Molière, Boileau, and Rousseau. Neither of these foreign countries provided a major source of material; he saw them as providing an alternative — and limited — way of launching ideas into the literary world. His genius was Spanish, his scope cosmopolitan. He obviously agreed with Tomás de Iriarte's observation in the last lines of his fable "Tea and Sage": "Any Spaniard who would recite / Five hundred lines of Boileau and Tasso, / May not even be aware or have in sight / The language written in by Garcilaso."

CHAPTER 4

The Two Masks of Drama

I *Laugh, Please, It's a Comedy*

"LACKS comic force";[1] "no interest, grace, or style";[2] "lacks interest";[3] "cold French tragedy *[sic]*";[4] "of entirely French cut";[5] "wretched".[6] So critics have reacted to Moratín's first play, written in 1762 "at Montiano's request."[7] In many ways the criticism is valid; there is much to complain of in this work. But there is also a sizable amount of interesting material, well-handled scenes, and amusing characterizations, which, under the right director's hand and the properly serious attitude of the acting company, might have carried the play through a moderately successful run. As it was, it was never performed.[8]

The influence of Lope, Calderón, Moreto, and Tirso on this comedy is so evident that, except for its adherence to the three Classical unities, its didactic bent, and the presence of that very eighteenth-century phenomenon, the petimetra, the play could have been written in Spain's seventeenth century. The plot, full of tricks, hidden boyfriends, love-at-first-sightings, lovers' plaints, threatened duels, and the like, is strictly a residue of the efforts of the playwrights of the previous century. The servants parallel the love affairs of their masters. There are asides, mistaken identities, narrow escapes, ill-guarded secrets, and confusions which need to be sorted out at the end. The servants are full of wily cunning. They squabble comically. Pedigrees of nobility are important. True love is rewarded, and three marriages set everything right as the play draws to a close. It is, in short, a comic honor play, supposedly updated to meet the new aesthetic concerns of the Neoclassicists.

Moratín was conscious of the shadows of Lope and Calderón that hovered over him. He did not attempt to break away from their influence, but merely to create a play that avoided the excesses of dramaturgy that were so disturbing to him. In his final argument

125

concerning which of the girls he should marry, the main character, Félix, says to his friend Damián:

> ¿Por ventura os acordáis,
> Que de ella me hicisteis hoy
> Una arenga tan famosa,
> Que pareció relación
> De don Pedro Calderón,
> Alabándola de hermosa?[9]

> (By chance do you recall
>   That about her today you gave me
>   Such a remarkable harangue
>   That it seemed to be a tale
>   By don Pedro Calderón
>   Praising her beauty?)

Nothing bitter or hostile is evident in the reference. If imitation is the greatest form of praise, then Moratín's praise of the Spanish *comedia* runs high in this work. Line after line conjurs up images of Lope's flights of fancy, Calderón's clever structures, or Moreto's sly wit, but only images, to be sure. Moratín's gifts could not approximate those of his predecessors, yet the points of contact with the past are numerous. Speeches echo familiar words from other plays, or pick up the tone of well-known scenes. Segismundo's bitter realization that birth itself is a crime can be heard in María's "Is it a crime to love?" (73). Federico rescued Cassandra from an accident and immediately fell in love with her in Lope's *El castigo sin venganza* (Punishment Without Revenge); we learn that Félix had once saved María from "that danger" in Valladolid, precipitating their mutual love (79; Moratín), true to his aesthetic demands, though, has the scene narrated instead of dramatized, as Lope had done). María's aside "Heavens above! I am doomed" (71) reminds us of Mencía's "You can't leave (I'm doomed)" taken from Calderón's *El médico de su honra* (The Physician of His Honor). The dramatic language of the seventeenth century was a part of Moratín's early dramatic creations. Certain stylistic devices favored in the Golden Age (i.e., symmetry and enumeration) are used in *La petimetra,* but without the symbolic impact or the poetic craft displayed in that earlier period.[10]

The plot is a shifting and amusing lovers' rectangle: Damián loves Jerónima, the silly petimetra, whose sensible cousin María loves the noble Félix; Félix loves Jerónima at first, but soon realizes her superficiality and declares for María — however, not before Damián learns that the 17,000-*ducat* dowry belongs not to Jerónima but to María, who is now suddenly the object of his own undying love. Félix and Damián are acquaintances or friends, depending on the current state of their amorous competitions, and both are constantly avoiding the protective machinations of the girls' uncle, Rodrigo, who reads his law books and dithers. A supporting trio of agreeable servants rounds out the eight-character cast. The characterizations are interesting, if not wholly believable in their rapid emotional changes.

Doña Jerónima, the vain and frivolous petimetra, is positively awful as a person, and we laugh at her idiocies even as we recognize Moratín's two-pronged satire: the ridicule of that specific social type, the petimetra, and the satire of the vain foibles and weaknesses in us all. Her type, in fact, became a popular target for dramatic parody in the 1760s and 1770s, particularly by Moratín's literary enemy, Ramón de la Cruz. Moratín himself criticized the foolishness of the petimetra in his first poetic satire, published in the third issue of the *Poet:*

> ¿No ves que el no saber, ni aun una letra,
> En las damas es hoy lo que mantiene
> El aire de presunción de petimetra,
>   Y en su conversación a cuento viene
> Solo el corsé, la bata o la basquiña,
> Que la amiga prestada o propia tiene?
>   ¿No ves que no hay quien su desorden riña,
> Por no desazonar, como ellos dicen,
> Los chistosos gracejos de la niña?
>   ¿Que aguantan que su cuerpo martiricen
> La cotilla, el zapato, el sofocante,
> Hasta que de apretados se destricen?
>   ¿No ves que el que se precia de su amante
> Por méritos alega monerías,
> Para que en sus favores adelante?
>   Esceden en suspiros a Macías,
> Hacen vil profesión de lisonjeros,
> Y así pasan las noches y los días. (BAE, 31)

> (Don't you see that knowing nothing, not even a letter,
> In a lady is today what maintains
> Her airs and appearance as a petimetra,

And in her conversation the only relevant thing
Is the corset, the housecoat, and the petticoat,
Either borrowed from a friend or her own?
    Don't you see that nobody reprimands her disorder
Not to make tasteless, as they say,
The "witty jests of the girl."
    That they tolerate the martyrdom of their body
To the corsets, shoes, and neck ribbons
Until nearly overcome with the squeezing?
    Don't you see that he who thinks he's her lover
Must speak continuous foolishness,
In order to advance in her favors?
    They have more sighs than Macías,
They are professional flatterers
And that's how they spend night and day . . . .)

Other writers took the same stance. Torres Villarroel gives a wonderful satirical sketch of the petimetra's masculine counterpart in his poem "Ciencia de los cortesanos de este siglo" (The Science of Courtly Gentlemen in This Century) and in the *Visiones,* where a whole chapter is devoted to the petimetre. Tomás de Iriarte matches it in his witty sonnet "Tres potencias bien empleadas en un caballerito de este tiempo" (Three Powers to be Well Used by a Gentleman of Today).[11]

Jerónima is an amusing character. The only thing she does in the course of the entire play is get dressed (this takes two acts), take a stroll to Mass, and come home to change clothes again. She is utterly useless, demanding, deceitful, and periodically cranky. She is not even particularly good-looking, although she sees herself as the picture of fashion, and confirms this judgment by frequent consultations with her well-worn mirror. She takes the negative epithet of petimetra, which everyone calls her behind her back, as a high compliment and a recognition of her chic. Her sole concerns are which dress (really, which artful disguising of the same couple of dresses with ribbons and adornments, since she is poor) and hairstyle to put on today. We easily feel superior to her since her faults are obvious; in fact, she shows them, talks about them, and if that were not clear enough, Moratín repeatedly points them out through the other characters. We are never unaware that Moratín is in control of his presentation of her and is conscious of his characterization. Ana, whose only task is to comb Jerónima's hair, elicits this comment from Jerónima herself: "What foolishness is in the

air / In this contradictory century / That I pay this girl a salary /
Just because she combs my hair!'' (68). At a later point Moratín
has Félix comment:

> ¡Válgame Dios! ¿Qué he de hacer
> En un lance tan estraño?
> Si lo que a mí me sucede
> Se fingiera en un teatro,
> Lance propio de comedia
> Lo juzgara el vulgo vano. (81)

> (Good Heavens! What am I to do
>   In such a strange situation?
>   If what is happening to me
>   Took place in a theater
>   The vain public would judge it
>   A good plot for a comedy.)

The play serves as a bridge from the wild abandon (in Moratín's
opinion) of Golden-Age dramaturgy to the carefully controlled
Neo-classical ideal later perfected by Nicolás's son Leandro. Even
the theme previews Leandro's *El sí de las niñas* (When a Girl Says
Yes) when Nicolás demonstrates the foolishness of a lack of proper
education and serious approach to one's life in society. María
captures the author's stance when she answers Jerónima's accusation that she would have her cousin go about sloppy and dirty:

> M.   No quiero nada
>   Entendámonos, mujer,
>   Que un medio se ha de escoger
>   . . .
> J.   Pues, ¿qué tienes que notar?
> M.   El esceso.   (68–9)

> (M.   I want nothing.
>   Let's get one thing straight,
>   That one must choose a middle ground
>   . . .
> J.   Well, what's bothering you?
> M.   Excess.)

It is that "middle ground" which Moratín seeks, and he remains
critical of overkill, exaggeration, "excess." His satire of
Jerónima's excesses brings to mind his son's treatment of the outra-

geous Doña Irene — Jerónima's spiritual daughter — whose frivolity and flighty mercenary tendencies make us laugh so much in Leandro's masterpiece.

Minor autobiographical elements appear in Moratín's depiction of Félix, who, like the author, studied in Valladolid and is relatively new to Madrid, although not a total stranger (69). The scene reminds us of similar exchanges carried on in the "Eclogue to Velasco and González". Rodrigo, the uncle, is a lawyer, Moratín's own second profession. And Moratín's treatment of women tends toward a faint misogyny; the women control the situation, but through ingenuity and deceit, and they are aware of it. María's complaint that men "say what they want, / And whatever they want they do!" (73) is met with a cold command to shut up since, as Uncle Rodrigo icily tells her, philosophical questions are not for her.

La petimetra is not a bad play; it is pleasant to read and could be mildly entertaining if staged properly. There is dramatic interest, even if it is predictable. The characters are shallow, but amusing. The moral message is clear, and the exaggerations are pardonable in comedy. The comedy itself is broad, often strained, but often enchanting. Scenes like the one where Damián is busy flattering Jerónima while she, paying no attention to his verbal excess, chastises the hairdresser for pulling and pinching her hair (Act 1, Scene 2), work quite well. Moratín's parody of the Golden Age to-be-or-not-to-be speeches (3,9) is at times as funny as Leandro's dazzling put-down of dramaturgy gone crazy in *La comedia nueva* (The New Comedy).

Yet the play's defects are numerous enough to explain its failure. Some of the speeches are too long: Félix's fifth intervention runs to over 100 verses, and María is often plagued with the same gift of long gab. More accomplished playwrights might have dramatized these discourses, but from Moratín's viewpoint they were a dramatic asset since they helped to avoid any lapses in the unities.[12] Several of the entrances and exits are handled clumsily and are mere pretexts to change people. The exclusive use of eight-syllable *redondillas* and ballad forms (some also too long) detracts from the play's potential diversity. Periodically the rhyme scheme is imperfect (pages 67, 68, 76) or strained (83), although he does handle rhyme quite well: for example, the long a-o ballad in Act 1 (69–73) uses only forty-eight repeated words in the 598 verses; but by Act 3 too many rhymes begin to be repeated.

Many questions come to mind. Is María, whose first words to Jerónima are a brusque clarification of just who has money and who does not, and who lies to her uncle, the paragon of virtue that Moratín sets her up to be? Would the servant Roque barge into the room demanding payment for the laundress? Does anyone just walk into the intimate chambers of young ladies? Is it decorous to have the maid announce that she is picking lice from herself in the next room? Is it believable that Roque and Rodrigo are on stage together without being aware of the other's presence (a favorite Golden-Age stage trick; at least Leandro later handled such scenes in the dark[13])? Is it dignified for Rodrigo to threaten to break his nieces' heads should anyone disturb his books? Where did the orphaned girls really come from (Rodrigo's explanation is fuzzy and unconvincing, almost an afterthought)? How is it that Rodrigo does not know that Jerónima cannot cook, and must be told so by María? Where did the letter which Jerónima produces in the end (an *epistola ex machina*?) to prove Damián's intention to marry her come from, and why wasn't it produced before? How do the young men get into the house without the uncle's knowledge (he is very vigilant, we are told)? Would Félix, in the space of a few minutes, enter the house, meet Jerónima, fall madly in love with her, confront Damián, and threaten to duel with him? Do we really need the characters' announcements that they are alone ("Am I alone?" "Goodbye, I remain alone." "Alone I stand, I am alone." "Now that I am alone . . . "), when it is perfectly obvious they are? These are valid questions, since Moratín vociferously insisted that the rules, verisimilitude, and decorum were the fundamental demands of good theater. There was a disparity between his theory of drama and his practice of it.

Ironically it is the rules that ultimately defeat him in this first attempt at playwriting. Luzán and Corneille at least permitted the unity of place to include an entire city and its surroundings, but Moratín's play takes place in one single room "and it does not move a step from there, not even to the next room and this is what really should be called unity of place."[14] He is also stricter than Aristotle with the unity of time; where the ancient master grants a full day, Moratín's is more "natural," that is, it will take place within the three hours needed to perform the play. These restrictions appear to be artificial, and the dramatic strains produced enable us to fault the author on aesthetic grounds.

That theater was to be the school of good moral values is demonstrated in the patent lesson spoken in the last lines. After Jerónima has been symbolically defrocked and exposed as foolish, all the other cast members leave us with this thought: "And anyone who may imitate her, / . . . / Will end up in the same sorry state / As ended up the petimetra" (84). Hartzenbusch very rightly questions the propriety of Jerónima's going off to Mass draped on the arm of her current beau, hardly a suitable example of good behavior which the theater was supposed to reflect.[15] On his way toward this obvious didacticism, Nicolás created a hybrid play (which Leandro severely criticized[16]), a comedy that in essence maintained the internal freedoms of the Golden Age while it adhered to certain of the new Neoclassical principles. It becomes so obvious that Moratín is more heavily influenced by Spanish models than by French ones that we must wonder how he has been so unfairly characterized. The petimetra is a French type, to be sure, a woman who follows the current fashions from north of the Pyrenees, yet Moratín is merciless in his condemnation of her style, her emptiness, and her moral vacuity. Moratín, Francophile? Hardly.

Moratín apparently composed two more comedies during his lifetime, neither of which remains extant. We know nothing about his other attempted satire, *El ridículo don Sancho* (Ridiculous Don Sancho), mentioned by his friend Signorelli.[17] Of the rapidly composed *La defensa de Melilla* (The Defense of Melilla) we know only that he wrote it in 1775 to celebrate the intended defeat of Moroccan troops by Spanish soldiers. The Duke of Medinasidonia, one of those who encouraged Moratín to write the work, predicted that it would be a "monster of art," full of the "fantasy, the diction, the sonority of Lope, since it may not be possible to find in it the regularity of Racine,"[18] a most unusual statement to make to a man who was the supposed leader of the exclusively French Neoclassical school of writing, and implacable enemy of Lope. Clearly, Moratín was less a standard-bearer for French playwriting than has been previously alleged.

II *A Tragedy, But Not Tonight:* Lucrecia

Moratín's second play centers on a woman also, but of a very different type. Lucretia, the title character from this tragedy, written early in 1763,[19] is to be pitied, not ridiculed. The theme of conjugal fidelity is established in Tarquino's opening tirade on the sinful and lascivious behavior of Roman wives, who are openly unfaithful while their husbands are off at war. Lucretia is honest and prudent, but also beautiful and, after all, a woman; the faith in her of her husband, Colatino, is not swayed by Tarquino's suspicions, although it is his blind innocence that will contribute to the ultimate tragedy as Tarquino's lust for Lucretia precipitates the tragic denouement. When Tarquino, as emperor-to-be, claims his rights to everything in Rome and rapes Lucretia, she feels that her only course of action is suicide and neither the pleas of her husband and father nor their "forgiveness" of her sullied honor can dissuade her. Her suicide by stabbing turns the rest of the characters into an instant vigilante group as they extract the bloody dagger from the dead Lucretia and plunge it repeatedly, as the senators did to another Roman, Julius Caesar, into the vile Tarquino. This is to serve as our "escarmiento" (warning, 117). Where is reason? Where is rationality? Where is discourse? Where is a respect for the law? The ultimate tragedy is that Lucretia need not have killed herself. We find her more stupid than trapped in an inexorable web of tragic circumstances. Besides, Tarquino had told his servant Mevio of his lascivious intentions; Mevio told Fluvia, Tarquino's secret lover; Fluvia told Claudia, Lucretia's and Fluvia's friend; Claudia told her lover Valerio . . . and yet nobody told Lucretia or Colatino. Six out of the ten characters are party to the conspiracy that Moratín also sets up symbolically as the rape of Rome. Are we to believe this? Do these characters merit our anxiety or preocupation?

From the beginning we know what the outcome will be in this five-act play, and hence we must look for the work's virtues in places other than plot development. If the ending is predictable, then the author must capture our interest with moving speeches, fascinating characters, or intriguing structures which enable us to purge ourselves of pity engendered for the characters and to feel release and moral uplift. Lucretia's situation as the faithful wife who is severely wronged by the evil Tarquino should engender such release. But it does not. Moratín never manages to make the ten characters in this play anything less than one-dimensional puppets whose actions are not only predictable but also boring. We do not care what happens to them and the tragedy therefore collapses from within. Lucretia herself will serve as an example. She laments, complains, suffers, and frets so much that her "woe-is-me" posture becomes tiresome. She complains that her beloved Colatino is not with her (103), yet the moment he appears she exchanges three sentences with him and then retires to "thank the sainted gods." By Act 2 she is complaining that his stay will be too short. Why isn't she with him instead of merely grousing? When she is on stage, which is rare, she does nothing but complain. She does not have a good scene until Act 4, Scene 2, when she is warding off Tarquino's advances. The scene is both amusing and dramatically tense as Tarquino declares his love for her; but her innocence is such that she does not comprehend what he is telling her and it takes her so long to catch on that we begin to suspect that she is more dense than naive, and our concern for her weakens substantially.

Structurally there are similarities with *La petimetra,* although Moratín has succeeded in tightening his control of the material to excise many of the more flagrant violations of his own Neoclassical precepts. Many of the questions raised in the analysis of that comedy can be raised here as well. A few Golden-Age elements remain. Moratín is faithful to the Golden-Age honor code: "The vile Tarquino / Will die of Colatino's fury, / And I shall wash away your stain with his blood" (115). He even paraphrases Segismundo's famous "Nothing seems just / Which goes against my wishes" when one of Tarquino's men says to him: "Anything a prince may wish, / Sir, is lawful" (105). We may remember that Francisco de Rojas wrote a play based on *Lucrecia y Tarquino,* and Calderón himself referred to the theme in *La dama duende* (The Phantom Lady, Act 1, Scene 1).

As in his first play, Moratín has two men come into town after having been away. One is foolish or evil (Damián/Tarquino) while one is noble and good (Félix/Colatino). They appear in a lady's antechamber; talk of loves; and hide. An old man (Rodrigo/Tripciano — Lucretia's father) guards and advises the women. Their servants act as confidants and go-betweens. Misunderstandings arise, but of course the outcome in *Lucrecia* is not the comic round of marriages offered in *La petimetra.* Entrances and exits are still handled clumsily, and the play suffers from a lack of focus. It veers uncomfortably from being, on the one hand, rigidly academic and intellectual, and on the other, wildly exclamatory, laden with inappropriate or unbelievable behavior, even in "repressed" eighteenth-century Spain. And like the first play it was never staged. Leandro, calling it "admirable due to its regularity [attention to the rules]"[20] tried to suggest that it never saw full production because "the theater, tyrannized in those days by stupid poetasters, controlled by actors of the most depraved tastes, and supported by an insolent and foolish public, only nourished itself on absurdities."[21] This is plainly untrue. The play failed because it was bad.

Moratín's clearest model for this effort was the example set by his friend and mentor Montiano, whose two tagedies of the past decade, *Virginia* and *Ataúlfo,* were to be the standard models for Neoclassical tragedy in Spain. Moratín sought inspiration in a real tale, chronicled in various sources and treated by numerous authors (it was popular with Italian Renaissancee poets and artists, and even more so with Spanish Renaissance and Golden-Age authors[22]), and attempted to present a serious theme in a form which he considered elegant and dignified. He eschewed the light and popular ballads and *redondillas* that had served him in his comedy, selecting instead stately hendecasyllables in blank verse interspersed with rhymed couplets, which by general agreement were more befitting serious matters. But the line between stately and ponderous is a thin one indeed, one that Moratín transgressed more often than he intended.

The drama is not without merit. Moratín's success is primarily historical — his attempt at tragedy written in the regulated Neoclassical mode helped to initiate a national debate on the uses and abuses of theater. *Lucrecia* contains some dramatic highlights. Lucretia's initial lament is both moving and universal:

> ¡Ay de la esposa ausente e infelice,
> Cuyo consorte en la enemiga tierra
> Sufre el rigor de la espantosa guerra
> Al frente de contrarios tan feroces
> Solo por ensalzar la patria! ¡Oh dioses!
> ¡Santos genios domésticos! ¡Oh Lares!
> ¡Oh deidades de Roma titulares!
> Avasallad las bárbaras naciones,
> Que su yugo resisten, no los nobles
> Lechos desamparéis de las romanas,
> Que en triste viudedad temiendo viven. (103)

> (Woe is the absent and unhappy wife
>   Whose consort in enemy lands
>   Suffers the severity of frightful war
>   Withstanding ferocious adversities
>   Only to glorify his country! Oh, Gods!
>   Holy household spirits! Oh, Lar!
>   Oh titled deities of Rome!

Subdue the barbarous nations
That resist the yoke, do not forsake
The noble beds of Roman wives
Who live fearfully in sad widowhood.)

The play is full of sage advice, moral admonitions, and warnings of the dangers of arbitrary absolutism (with no contemporary political implications[23]), and it contains one of the characteristics of Moratín's writings that will become more and more evident as he continues his writing career — his intense patriotism. The play teems with patriotic sentiments and bombastic statements on the glory of his fatherland. It is a deep feeling that Moratín will display in practically every writing from 1763 until the end of his life. Moratín employs a device that would also be used, at his request, by Ignacio López de Ayala in the name of "good taste" — the bloody death of Lucretia takes place off stage (it is an idea taken directly from Luzán) and we are spared the violent horrors of her demise. Ayala eliminated his armless children from the *Numancia destruida* (Numancia Destroyed) at Moratín's suggestion, who deemed it inappropriate to show such extravagant behavior on stage. But then we know Lucretia has killed herself — we hear her cries of death ("Oh, I am dead!" 115), so we hardly need Claudia's forty-five-verse discourse detailing the act. And ironically Tarquino's even bloodier death takes place *on* stage. Again, contradictions abound.

Lucrecia received some attention in the press. Miguel de la Barrera, writing in the *Aduana Crítica* in 1763, focused his attention on the play in a twenty-nine-page article. He seems at first to be willing to support Moratín's attempt, but his analysis reveals the weaknesses of the play in some detail including the lack of strict historical authenticity, the inattention to form and versification ("the unities are not observed with all the precision that the author claims"), the inverisimilitude of the plot and of the tragic denouement. It is not a particularly profound or stinging criticism, but Moratín was sufficiently offended by it and by another written by one Mr. Flores[24] to get his friend Ignacio Bernascone to respond seven years later in the prologue he wrote for Moratín's next play, *Hormesinda*.

III *Oh, Nicolás! Oh, Hormesinda!*

By 1770 Moratín had learned his craft better. He also felt himself to be on surer ground since the Neoclassical campaigns for theatrical reform seemed to be gathering positive results. More translations were being done at the Royal Sites; there was more rewriting of older plays; and a few authors were about to try their hands at original regulated dramas. The next few years would witness the appearance of Cadalso's *Sancho García,* Ayala's *Numancia destruida,* and García de la Huerta's *Raquel.* It did not hurt their cause that they enjoyed official patronage and protection by the king's minister Aranda. Still, the year — 1770 — and the play — *Hormesinda* — are unanimously credited with beginning a renaissance of Spanish theater in the eighteenth century.[25]

Hormesinda is significantly more accomplished than *La petimetra* or *Lucrecia,* although not necessarily the result of more reflection or polish. Bernascone reveals that Moratín wrote the last three acts (more than half the play) in just four days, "interrupted often by my conversation, and by that of other friends."[26] It has deservedly received the most critical attention of Moratín's four plays. For this play Moratín learned to be less esoteric, less abstract than he had been in *Lucrecia.* He chose a theme familiar to the people, one that was capable of engendering their passion and their concern. The Pelayo theme had been brought to the public's attention in the last decade in an epic poem by Alonso de Solís[27] and Moratín picked it up and cloaked it in his Neoclassical mantle. He did permit more people on stage, Cantabrian and Asturian troops, a "large accompaniment" of Moors, more color and noise — in short, more interesting activity to support the wordy remonstrations of the central figures. He reached back into the dramatic past — his own, his country's, and the world's — for his newest tragedy.

He reused elements from his first tragedy: the tyrant (Tarquino/Munuza), who rapes or threatens the innocent heroine (Lucretia/Hormesinda), who is in turn protected by a wise elder (Triciptino/Trasamundo), and defended by a noble hero (husband Colatino/brother Pelayo). From Spain's past he took the outlines of the plot, and skillfully mixed it with the patriotic sentiments which the efforts of Pelayo to recapture Spain from the Moors always managed to stir up. From his country's literary past, as he had done before, he took snippets of emotion or imagery from Golden-Age plays: Munuza's claim, "I shall be the new fright of Spain" (86), recalls Aureliano's oath in Calderón's *La gran Cenobia* (Great Cenobia) to be "the bloody scourge and mortal fright of the land," and the final scene of *Hormesinda,* which depicts Munuza's head being borne aloft at the end of a lance, certainly recalls the bloody end of Lope's *Fuenteovejuna.* We are somewhat surprised at this concession to gross spectacle, which Moratín claimed to have opposed.

From world literature he borrowed from Shakespeare, creating his own brand of Hispanized *Othello.* His play contains the black intruder (Munuza/Othello), the innocent lady (Hormesinda/Desdemona), the evil counselor (Tulga/Iago), the contemplated murder, and even the falsified documents indicating infidelity. The endings are very different, of course; Shakespeare's is a true tragedy. Desdemona dies innocent, the result of confused and evil complications, while in Moratín's play everything works out in the end — the truth of Hormesinda's fidelity and honesty is confirmed, and the nasty Munuza receives his deserved punishment. Christian troops rush in at the last moment from practically nowhere to slay the Moorish usurpers, and Hormesinda is saved. Hormesinda's planned death is a result of Pelayo's stupidity, arrogance, and false sense of loyalty, but tragedy is averted when the dense Pelayo finally hears what everyone else has known all along — Hormesinda is innocent, the papers are false, Munuza is not a friend, and it was all a vicious conspiracy to subjugate Pelayo. Perhaps the actor Espejo's suggestion that Moratín add a pair of *graciosos* was not such a bad one after all.[28]

Technically, Moratín has achieved greater stability here than before, although the restrictions of time, place, and action still betray him. Entrances and exits are handled, for the most part, with more skill. The hendecasyllables yield more satisfying couplets, *cuartetos,* and *cuartetas* than in his previous attempt. The characters take on shades of color. Munuza, the best example, is not a black-and-white cardboard cutout, but a man blinded by passion into acting unwisely. He is not totally evil and consequently tiresome, but the shadows of his personality at times reveal a sensitive, and certainly clever, antihero. Pelayo, by contrast, looks pale and foolish, much too willingly seduced by Munuza's remonstrations of friendship, much too ready to believe the unproven accusations of infidelity against Hormesinda. He does not question Munuza's motives until Act 3, Scene 3 — much too late. Pelayo never confronts Hormesinda or reasons with her; even her clear statements of the wrong being done her fall on infuriatingly deaf ears. His sole approach to the problem is to abuse her and vow her death. He is far from the ideal brother, prince, and future leader of his country; only because a tragedy is averted and good ostensibly triumphs over evil do we forgive or rather forget his ludicrous behavior. His rapid changes in emotion are disquietingly abrupt; he appears unstable and certainly unfit to rule with temperance. If Moratín meant *Hormesinda* to be an exaltation and a justification of the benefits of enlightened despotism, he would have done better to have been more aware of the flaws in Pelayo's character, whom he sets up as the noble defender of family, state, and religion. Is Pelayo prepared to sell out, to betray his sister in exchange for some trappings of power?

> P.   Ya está dada
>   La sentencia fatal.
> M.   ¡Cuán generoso
>   Es tu pecho, Pelayo! ¡Qué glorioso
>   Te veré sin tal mancha! Amigo digno
>   De Munuza, y entonces en tus sienes
>   Pondré (mi juramento te lo abona)
>   De Asturias y Cantabria la corona. (95)

> (P.   The final sentence
>   Is already given.
> M.   How generous your
>   Breast is, Pelayo! How glorious
>   I shall see you without that stain! Friend
>   Worthy of Munuza, and then on your brow
>   I shall place [I swear it]
>   The crown of Asturias and Cantabria.)

Surely this is not Moratín's intention, but it is the effect on the spectator, and the high noble drama successfully established at many points in the play collapses. It should be recognized that Moratín cleverly sets up Trasamundo, through a misunderstanding between him and Pelayo, to support unwittingly Pelayo's accusations, but again it is Pelayo's haste — he tends to jump to conclusions — which works against his sister.

Still, it is an overwhelmingly Christian and patriotic play, whose elements prefigure the intensely traditional works of the sort of Romanticism exemplified by Agustín Durán, Gil y Zárate, Roca de Togores, Rivas, and Zorrilla. The monarchy is exalted, defended, and unquestioned ("A king of Spain is more a father than a king," 97). Hormesinda is devoutly Spanish:

> ¿Quién me lo dijera
> A mí, cuando el obsequio desdeñaba
> De tanto conde godo; cuando fiera
> Despedí esposos nobles de la Galia,
> Y me negué a los príncipes de Italia? (85)

> (Who would have said it to me,
>   To me, when I rejected the flattery
>   Of so many Gothic counts; when I fiercely
> Sent away noble suitors from Gaul,
>   And I denied my favors to Italian princes?)

She is Christian, and the blessed virtues of that religion are pitted against the "vile" and "treacherous" infidels. She is haughty, and predictably anti-Semitic:

> ¿Y cómo era posible que pensara
> Un moro vil, infame y atrevido,
> Entre tostados árabes nacido,
> Llegar a consentir fuera su esposa
> La hermana de Pelayo?
> . . .
> ¿Cómo aspirar a ser mi esposo pudo
> Quien no merece ser esclavo mío?
> . . .
> Yo, española y cristiana. (85)

> (And how was it possible that a vile,
>   Infamous and daring Moor, born
>   Among toasted Arabs, should think
> That the sister of Pelayo
>   Would consent to be his wife?
> . . .
> How could he aspire to be my husband
> He who does not deserve to be my slave?
> . . .
> I, a Spaniard and a Christian.)

Cadalso's María Ignacia Ibáñez must have been lovely in the role she played from February 12 to 17 at the Príncipe Theater. Her skills would have helped pass over or soften the unending stream of questions and exclamations that Moratín wrote into her part. When it was performed, notwithstanding Leandro's claims that it was staged solely due to a campaign of support encouraged by Aranda, and notwithstanding the play's drawbacks, we can believe that it enjoyed a modest success. The receipts were not bad; the six-day run pulled in 19,000 *reales,* just a few thousand less than the annual salary of the director of the Madrid theaters.[29] This median intake of over 3,150 *reales* per day was actually rather good, considering that, in previous years, the plays of Calderón himself were attracting ridiculously small audiences, with median intakes of 731 and 887 *reales.*[30] Juan Ponce's company of actors was well known and relatively professional,[31] having acted in many of the "enemy" Cruz's *sainetes.* Vicente Merino's Pelayo must have stirred the hearts of his countrymen as he related his travails in Cordoba in a long (154 verses) and declamatory speech, an embryonic epic poem full of lively action and interesting descriptions that remind us of the colorful "Bullfight Festival" and the descriptive elements of "Cortés's Ships Destroyed." Pelayo's uplifting patriotic statements make him the focal point of the two levels of the play — the personal enslavement and betrayal of Hormesinda vs. the political enslavement and betrayal of Christian Spain — and Pelayo will be the key figure in liberating both his sister and his country. Once his sister is safe (her chains are symbolically broken), he marches off to Covadonga, site of the beginning of the Christian Reconquest, and then off to reclaim Spain.

Such stirrings of patriotic sentiment were much in vogue with the authors of the Neoclassical plays. *Sancho García, Numancia Destroyed, Raquel,* Jovellanos's play on the Hormesinda theme, *Pelayo* (written in 1769[32]), and Moratín's own *Guzmán el Bueno,* all mined the nationalistic lode with varying degrees of success. Even the Italians, with whom Moratín had always had an interestingly symbiotic relationship, began to look back to Spain for inspiration, and an *Ormesinda* was produced in Italy in 1783. Spanish Neoclassicists all responded to a real need, a growing national consciousness, witnessed by the fact that it was during Carlos III's reign that the Spanish flag and the national anthem were made official.[33] The printed version of *Hormesinda* received some attention, supported with praises written by Moratín's friends Bernascone, Juan de Iriarte, Conti, and Gómez Ortega. Juan Peláez wittily viewed these Latin and Italian inscriptions as gravestones, marking the early death of "Madame Tragedy,"[34] so hostile was his reaction to Moratín's play. Bernascone's prologue, in contrast, was positively rapturous in its praise, sure that Moratín, whom he suggested is ignored or vilified now, will be vindicated by history and recognized as a great author.[35] He takes it as an undeniable achievement that *Hormesinda* "is a tragedy without love, without strange episodes, without soliloquies, without asides, without leaving the theater empty from the beginning to the end . . . . "[36] He becomes the voice for what is in fact Moratín's most notable achievement: that the play is not a translation nor a reworking of an older play, but that it is an original drama and based on a theme indigenous to Spain. Inspired by models, it should become a model itself.

Not everyone agreed with Bernascone's high opinion of *Hormesinda.* Juan Peláez certainly did not, and he published his fifty-five-page *Reparos sobre la tragedia intitulada* Hormesinda, *y contra su Prólogo* (Observations on the Tragedy Entitled Hormesinda, and Against Its Prologue) in 1770 to prove it, accusing Bernascone of writing not a prologue but a panegyric. He does support the fact that *Hormesinda* was received "with so much acclaim," while sarcastically attacking Bernascone's prejudiced arrogance and overblown claims. He demolishes Bernascone's braggadocio cited above, stating the obvious — that love does play a part in the work: "The tragedy's author confesses the existence of Munuza's love: the commentator denies it."[37] He derides Moratín's use of the unities, his often imperfect rhymes, the liberties he takes with history, his concept of tragedy, and more. His criticisms are often right on target. Even Tomás de Iriarte, while ostensibly censuring Ramón de la Cruz, joined the clamor against *Hormesinda,* decrying its tortured plot and arguing convincingly that the play could have ended as early as Act 2, Scene 4, but does not, obviously because Moratín does not want it to.[38] His "Carta escrita al Pardo por un caballero de Madrid a un amigo suyo" (Letter Written to the Pardo [site of one of the Royal Theaters] by a Gentleman from Madrid to a Friend of His), underlines *Hormesinda*'s weaknesses while trying to pass them off as unimportant. With friends as unfaithful as Iriarte, Moratín hardly needed enemies like Ramón de la Cruz. Certainly we are not surprised at what Cruz, the leader of the opposite theatrical pack, wrote about Moratín's play:

After many months of effort, two of preparatory praises to get the people inflamed, one of rigorous rehearsal; and at last with three letters and a recommendation procedure, they presented to the world the monstrous and detested tragedy *Hormesinda.*[39]

He was right about its being detested in some circles. Even Iriarte confessed that everyone, the learned and the unschooled alike, hated it, and that rarely have "intellectuals and idiots" agreed on anything so unanimously.[40] But if we believe him, what are we to make of the ticket receipts?

As far as we know, nobody other than Bernascone came forth to defend *Hormesinda* in print, but its position as the first in a line of original tragedies attests to its historical importance. Again, imitation is the highest form of praise; but while Moratín's play was imitated by his Neoclassical friends, at the same time Cruz's plays were applauded by the people. And the most troubling question of all remains: why did so many people, everyone except Moratín and a limited band of followers, know the play was weak? Or did Moratín know and defend his intentions rather than his results? Iriarte suggests the latter was the case, writing of how he refused to listen to his friends' suggestions to improve the drama.[41] Moratín was his own Pelayo, refusing to accept the hints and statements of those around him; only this time no Cantabrian troops came to the rescue. It was a full five years before he undertook another playwriting challenge *(La defensa de Melilla)* and a full seven years before another one was published *(Guzmán el Bueno).*

IV *Kin or Country?:* Guzmán el Bueno

Guzmán el Bueno, written in 1777,[42] reflects that strong patriotism evident in *Hormesinda,* and like the previous work it is based on a real incident in Spanish history. His documentary source was the *Crónicas de los reyes de Castilla, desde Don Alfonso el Sabio hasta los Católicos Don Fernando y Doña Isabel* (Chronicles of the Kings of Castile, from Alfonso the Wise to the Catholics Fernando and Isabel). Here, however, Moratín was closer to his subject, the Guzmán family, headed by the Duke of Medinasidonia, who had been a friend and patron of Moratín for many years, and the play became an expression of gratitude for that support. The duke and duchess had long encouraged Moratín to continue to pusue his literary aims, involving him in poetry competitions and supporting his playwriting activities (Leandro cites his involvement with the Italian poet Talassi and with the Melilla play[43]). Moratín had praised the duke in an ode (BAE, 57) in which he called him "half of my soul." Medinasidonia himself was a minor literary adventurer as the author of some poetry and the translator of Racine's *Iphigénie.* Moratín's first play, *La petimetra,* was dedicated to the duchess, indicating a relationship which dated at least back to 1762. Later, Moratín dashed off a ballad, a rather successful one, to her husband.[44] In the prologue to *Guzmán,* Moratín once again directed his praise to the duke, whose noble ancestors embodied the patriotic spirit so impressive to him. It provided Moratín another forum to restate his quite unrevolutionary belief that obedience to higher authority is essential to man's happiness, and that it is a characteristic particularly evident in the Spanish temperament. He was, after all, raised under the good graces of the reigning family, and he viewed the enlightened monarchy with respect.

The prologue to *Guzmán,* after dispensing some gushing lines of praise to Medinasidonia, becomes a retrospective defense of Moratín's past endeavors in which he attempts to answer his critics. Although he appears painfully conscious of this drama's faults, he repeats his distaste for those Olympian critics and theorizers who pronounce upon creative works without attempting to produce any themselves. The prologue, though, surprises the individual familiar with Moratín's previous critical positions, for he has changed. Apparently stung by La Barrera's attack on his confusion of truth vs. verisimilitude, he now holds that dramatic and "physical" verisimilitude are not one and the same; that Nature, which was to be so slavishly imitated before, is actually a rather slippery ideal, one that changes with each author's perception of it. He even admits to the possibility that dramatic genius may skirt the rules for effect, since "the rules of art, like laws, cannot provide for all situations."[45]

He does not go so far as to apply this newly admitted freedom to himself, of course, because the rules are still essential, but his defense of the way he applies the three unities to *Guzmán* underlines his realization of the weakness of such restrictions. In fact, the single action is Guzmán's defense of Tarifa, the single time span is less than one day, and the setting is a split stage representing two distinct places! On one side is the Moorish encampment, and on the other are the walls of Tarifa, the city which Guzmán swears to defend to the death. Moratín rationalized this split away, writing nonsensically about the audience's sitting on the parapet of the city from where it can see and hear all the action. Had he merely accepted a break in that one unity, or an acceptance of an ancient ideal, we would credit him with the presentation of a modern stage technique, one used successfully even today. Perhaps we still can, since the refusal to switch from place to place forced him to solve the problem ingeniously, locating both camps on the same stage and carrying us from one to the other as the action demands. Granted, a literal interpretation of the unities permitted that of place to include the environs of a city, but Moratín had not been so inclined before. He becomes an easy target for criticism, though, through his stubborn refusal to admit to what he has done.

Moratín is aware of the historical and literary precedents of his drama ("I have seen some dramas with this plot"[46]), as he had been for *Lucrecia,* basing himself on the historical record while imbibing the examples of his literary predecessors. Surely he knew Luis Vélez de Guevara's *Más pesa el rey que la sangre* (The King Weighs More Than Blood); others included Juan Claudio de la Hoz y Mota's *El Abraham castellano* (The Spanish Abraham) and Antonio de Zamora's *El blasón de los Guzmanes* (The Glory of the Guzmans). In 1768, just nine years before Moratín's play, Cándido María de Trigueros wrote *Los Guzmanes o el cerco de Tarifa* (The Guzmans or the Siege of Tarifa), influenced by his participation in Olavide's Sevillian tertulia. Other authors were later to pick up the theme: Iriarte in dramas, Quintana in a poem, and Gil y Zárate in a play written when Romanticism was in full flower.

Gone is the polemical tone of Moratín's previous writing, replaced by a defeatist admission that the campaign to reform the theaters which he had so actively supported was a failure: "Well I know that this tragedy is not for today's theaters, where only abomination and barbarousness reign."[47]

Don Alonso Pérez de Guzmán, el Bueno, must choose between his son's life and his country's freedom. The infidel hoards, led by Jacob Aben Juseph (and portrayed as idiot lackeys, continually surprised by the virtue of Alonso), have captured Pedro, and the price for his safe return is the capitulation of Tarifa, the city held by Spanish troops. Naturally, in a blaze of heroic sentiment, Guzmán refuses, and neither the incessant tears of his wife, María, nor the plaints of his future daughter-in-law Blanca can force him to sell out his country ("Don't you know that the noble fortress / Is not mine, but rather my king's alone?" 121). The situation creates the possibility of intense drama, of a father's agonic choice between his flesh and blood and his country's expectations, and Moratín lifts the reader at times to heights of passion that give real force to the play, but which he is incapable of sustaining.

Doña María is another example of Moratín's inability to present

female characters convincingly. They are frivolous (Jerónima),
inept (Lucrecia), victimized (Hormesinda), or tearful (María), but
never very real. María's entire role consists of lamenting the antici-
pated loss of her son. She is overdrawn and predictable. Moratín
no doubt wishes to characterize her as the prototypical mother, but
he merely succeeds in creating a somewhat pathological blatherer
since she is willing to do anything to save her son. Handled
properly, she would be a tragic figure; as is, she is a nuisance. Even
Moratín's contemporaries recognized this clumsy presentation of
the hero's wife; says Sempere: " . . . In *Guzmán* the continuous
supplication of the weepy Doña María Coronel, who does not seem
to be the wife of a grandee and of a hero like Don Alfonso, far
from causing any emotion, first produces a dryness which is tiresome, and hardly enables us to finish reading the piece."[48] Guzmán
finally rants at her to shut up:

> ¿Qué blasfema tu voz? Viven los cielos,
> Que te abandonaré, doña María,
> Sin que el materno afecto te disculpe,
> Pues eres vulgar madre. ¿Cuál esposa
> A un hombre como yo tal decir osa?
> A Guzmán, que me corro, ¡vive el cielo!
> De mirarte a mi lado, ¿quién tal dice?
> ¿Esto se escucha entre cristianos? ¿Esto
> Las ricas fembras de Castilla piensan?
> ¿La gran consorte de Guzmán el Bueno? (139)

> (What blasphemies are these? By God,
> I will abandon you, María,
> With no concern for your maternal affections,
> Since you are a common mother. What wife
> Would dare to say such things to a man like me?
> To Guzmán, who is embarrased, my God!
> To see you at my side — who would say such things?
> Is this what one hears among Christians? Is
> This what the rich ladies of Castile think?
> The great consort of Guzmán the Brave?)

We get the feeling that this speech is Moratín's as well, and given
from the heart. Nowhere does Moratín create women *qua* women,
with sincere feelings, rational thoughts, or normal desires. Dorisa,
his one great love, is idealized, and the woman in *The Whores' Art,*
while treated rationally, are ultimately degraded in their function to
serve man's pleasures.

If Moratín set out to create the military equivalent of the perfect citizen, as Andioc suggests,[49] he fails miserably. Guzmán's above-cited speech reveals the flaw in his character — the impenetrable arrogance that prohibits him from truly agonizing over his situation. Moratín has made him too aware of his supposed bravery, telling us of his pain rather than showing it to us. From the first scene he demonstrates a singular lack of sympathy for his son, acting angry and critical of Pedro, whom he calls "rash" and "insolent" (118). We must question the sincerity of his painful remonstrations over the sacrifice of his son. We also question his judgment: he offers to give up anything he owns, including his estates in San Lúcar and Medinasidonia, to free his son, but he will never give up Tarifa, which is the king's property.

Granted the nobility of protecting the king's land at all cost, we still suspect the judiciousness of turning over Christian lands in the heart of Spain, even though they are privately owned, to the Moors. Those lands were, after all, the battlegrounds of the entire Reconquest. Could Guzmán be so ignoble as to trade it all away? And his sacrificing of his son for his country's honor loses its heroic dimensions when the Christian forces capture Aben-Jacob's daughter Fatima and he acts as heroically as Guzmán, likewise proffering a sacrifice. In the same vein, are we to believe that an unarmed young girl (Blanca) could slip into the enemy camp and into the intimate circle of Aben-Jacob unnoticed (134)? Are we to tolerate another rescue-at-the-last-minute (although they come too late to save Pedro's life) as we were forced to do in *Hormesinda*? Are we to be moved by meaningless banalities ("Lady, I was a son to my father / Before being a father to my son" 137)? Are we to be captivated by the endless talk, talk, talk of this play? Are we to sympathize with a man who, upon hearing that the recent noises were those accompanying the beheading of his son, responds: "I was afraid they were storming the fort" (140)? Modern theatergoers would surely reject such lapses; unfortunately for Moratín, so did those of his own day.

Perhaps these objections are too logical, too harsh. But it was Moratín himself who led the campaign for a reasonable and logical approach to drama. It was he who held verisimilitude as drama's major goal. It was he who deplored allegory for its illogic. So it is fair to judge him on the same grounds, and in many ways he comes off not too well. *Guzmán* was never performed, the third of his plays to suffer that fate. Leandro was asked to polish it up for a stage debut, but he decided against it and consequently it never had a theatrical run.[50] The critics, from Sempere on, have pointed to the play's unusual denouement, claiming that the unhappy ending, where vice seemingly reigns supreme and virtue goes unrewarded, is contrary to accepted practice in tragedy-writing. Pedro does die, Guzmán loses his son, and María remains frustrated and bitter, to be sure. But the play's point was not the family's happiness, but rather its sacrifice to the greater good, that of the State, and Guzmán's word of honor to the king. And in this light, the play ends exactly as Moratín wished it to; the integrity of Spanish territories and a nobleman's honor remain undamaged. That is the point, and in it, Moratín succeeds in meeting his goal. And, perhaps, Moratín is still more influenced by Golden-Age dramaturgy than he would like to admit, unconsciously following the examples of Lope and Calderón of subtly tracing the real sources of the tragic ending:[51] Don Alonso is, when carefully studied, less than a thoughtful and well-rounded human being. The association would have to have been unconscious on Moratín's part, of course, for it would not do to criticize one's patron. We do not know what the duke's response to the play was.

Guzmán was translated, or rather recast, into English in 1802.[52] The anonymous English translator, while attracted by the play's theme and presentation, could not resist the impulse to "improve" it, and two of Moratín's most cherished tenets — the decorous observation of the unities and the tragic denouement — disappear. In the new version the scenes change no fewer than fifteen times. Nor does Pedro die; he escapes dressed as a Moor and joins his father in the final battle. Pedro and "Blanche" live happily ever after. It would have been better had the Englishman merely added a pair of *graciosos*.

Yet if *Guzmán* is another example of Moratín's intense "Spanishness," the theme is the exaltation of Spanish patriotic duty and honor based on his own country's history and literature. Even though he still remains faithful to his break with the irregularity of the past theater by writing a regulated play, he is far from an imitator of foreign playwrights, French or otherwise. He carefully explains his position as a defender of the Spanish language, perhaps to answer those who had misinterpreted his goals and who were accusing him of literary treason. His goal will be, he emphasizes, to write in

pure Spanish, which is a virtue these days, having corrupted it so little . . . .
I am not sure I can do it, although I continually study it. This does not
mean I oppose the study of other languages, which should be known for
other things . . . but to achieve perfection in a foreign language, besides
being useless, is impossible . . . . [53]

His plays are not translations of foreign works, not foreign-
inspired, not foreign-dominated. They are intensely and defen-
sively Spanish, something which he evidently feels obliged to re-
emphasize: "I wish to be a noted antiquarian [of our ancestors'
customs], more than of those of other nations which interest us
little or not at all: I do not know if this patriotism is con-
demnable."[54]

V *Conclusion: Moratín and His Theater*

Moratín was committed to a higher degree of theatrical
standards than those in evidence in the 1760s and 1770s. To that
end he wrote a stream of critical observations in which he attempted to distinguish the qualities that made up good theater.
More than that, he wrote four dramas which were supposed to
reflect his ideals and become models for future theater-writing.
They succeeded at the former but failed at the latter.

Even so, I. McClelland correctly notes that a work that fails as
drama can be influential as theory.[55] Moratín helped to clarify what
was acceptable in theater by providing examples that were unacceptable. It was obviously not his goal to delineate the parameters
of quality drama by in essence defining its negative aspects, yet this
is precisely what happened. He was sensitive enough and sufficiently opinionated about what good theater should be that he must
have been aware of the weaknesses of his own plays. It is difficult
to imagine his being blind to the glaring inadequacies of those
efforts, yet we are at a loss to explain why he refused to correct
some of their obvious failings. Perhaps reflection and rewriting
were not at his command. We know he was a surprisingly fast
writer who tossed off the Melilla play in six hours and dashed off
the last acts of *Lucrecia* in two successive evenings. *Hormesinda* as
well was the product of a rapid pen, hardly "careful," as Ms.
McClelland would have it. It shows, and surprises, since Nicolás's
goals appeared to be thought, calm reflection, and the polishing of
one's works. Leandro certainly learned this lesson, and produced

the most successful Neoclassic play in Spanish history. His father ignored the lesson, but even so, Sempere cited *Hormesinda* and *Guzmán* as "examples of today's good taste,"[56] and the residual effects were felt for generations in Spain. Some careful reflection might have saved these plays from their contradictions and flaws. On the other hand, if the testimony recorded is correct as to the rapidity of his writing, we must remain astonished with that facility and only lament that he was not more careful when he put his theories into practice.

Not that the plays are horrible; they are just not that good. Perhaps Moratín even thought they were, but his constant apologies for them in his prologues seem to indicate otherwise. He lacked confidence in the effectiveness of a dramatic statement, often feeling the need to employ discourse and declamation to state the obvious. If La Barrera was correct when he wrote, "There are two effective ways of persuading any system — reason and example,"[57] then we can only suggest that, in drama, Moratín's strength lay with the former more than with the latter. Even Signorelli, who sympathized with Moratín's theoretical positions in theater, could not bring himself to write enthusiastically about his friend's four dramas. Full praise for Moratín's intentions and mild praise for some of his achievements were mixed with straightforward criticism of the weaknesses in the plays: tepid characterization, poor plotting, and lack of "energy."

Moratín, who was supposedly so chained to French and Italian influences, used no French or Italian characters in any of his plays; he only used one Frenchified type (the silly fashion-conscious girl in his first comedy), and then only to satirize her. His themes were Spanish — either taken from contemporary Spain *(La petimetra),* from Spain's heroic history *(Hormesinda, Guzmán el Bueno),* or themes widely treated by previous Spanish authors *(Lucrecia).* The numerous echoes of Golden-Age playwriting techniques are incidental but revealing. They show how fully steeped in Golden-Age literature Moratín was, unable to eschew completely the influence of his predecessors, no matter how much he protested their excesses. He was also heavily influenced by the older crowd in the early 1760s as he began his writing career. He was stricter then, less willing to translate his emotions into dramatic action. He believed that emotion was somehow contrary to reason and his plays contain warnings against violent passion and excess. But by the 1770s he was more comfortable with his emotional base. He began to establish his own identity, less rigid and more nationalistic. His crowd had changed too, from that of the stern Juan de Iriarte and Montiano to the witty, warm, and equally brilliant bunch that included Cadalso, Tomás de Iriarte, López de Ayala, and others mentioned in connection with the San Sebastián Inn. The change is noticeable in his plays.

That Moratín's plays are more criticized than read is evident from the absurdities that have been written about them. Of course, many of the critical observations are perceptive, but what are we to do with those who affirm, for example, that *Guzmán el Bueno*'s inherent Spanishness stems in part from the "prodigious" use of Spanish verse forms like the *redondilla,* the *lira,* the ballad, and "others,"[58] when in fact the play is written in a subtle pattern of hendecasyllabic free verse, at times employing asonantal rhyme, at times consonantal rhyme, periodically intercalating *cuartetas* and *pareados* into the rhythmic structure? There is not a ballad, *redondilla,* or *lira* in the entire play. Nor, as is now obvious, can we accept his being called "a furious enemy of our seventeenth-century theater."[59]

Moratín's plays were revolutionary in that they went against the popular grain in form, but their content was staunchly conservative. There are no hints of approval of rebellious activity or political unrest. The only battles he portrays are those to maintain the noble *status quo* against any foreign threats (foreign customs in *La petimetra,* foreign armies in *Lucrecia* and *Guzmán,* foreign lovers in *Hormesinda).* They are protective of government stability while upholding traditional values — the closeness of the family, the nobility of Christianity, kindness, conjugal fidelity (!), patriotic fervor, and above all, reason and the avoidance of excess.

CHAPTER 5

Summation: Neoclassical
Author, Spanish Patriot

MORATÍN was an author of impressive erudition who aspired to be useful to society and to the society of letters. His writings were produced in good faith, based on artistic and moral concerns. Like other writers of his day he did not care about popular appeal; he would reform, educate, and give culture to the people. Only, alas, the people did not want it, and the experiment proved to be a limited success. It was an enlightened despotism of the literary kind — literature for the people but without the people.

Moratín's literary theories — labeled since his time as those of Neoclassicism — gained the attention of numerous writers, while his poetry gained their respect. His dramas, on the other hand, faded into semioblivion: the only one to be staged, *Hormesinda,* achieved only moderate success and, indeed, attempts were made to reform *it* (that famous suggestion that he add a pair of *graciosos).* His dramatic technique might have improved if he had written more and seen more of his plays brought to life on the stage, from where he could mold the author's tricks to his reformist goals. But evidence suggests that tragedy was never a favorite forum for Spanish actors. As late as 1789, Díez González was still lamenting:

They still long for plays of magic and necromancy. They abhor tragedies and prefer those superficial comedies in which abound bravado, ostentation, duels, battles, and other such nonsense, and where they can show off by shouting, stamping their feet, and flapping their bones about.[1]

As a poet, Moratín was supremely talented; as a theorist, supremely opinionated and courageous; as a dramatist, supremely misguided. He was betrayed by his own animation, his impatience, and his refusal to heed his own belief that one should study, contemplate, write, and polish one's works to perfection. Perhaps he planned to edit and revise his works, plans interrupted by his untimely death, but he did publish his dramas which, while containing passages of disarming smoothness and beauty, are generally left in rather rough form.

Jean Jacques Rousseau's complaint that "nowadays there are no more Frenchmen, no more Germans, no more Spaniards, not even any Englishmen; despite what they say, there are only Europeans" was clearly not shared by Moratín. His ideas were conservative: he supported the monarchy and seemed as frightened by the prospects of social anarchy as he was angered by the reality of literary anarchy. He was a traditionalist firmly situated in the historical flow of Spanish culture, and so proud of that culture that he took issue with the thought that foreigners considered any aspect of it backward or uncivilized. He may not have agreed with Vicente García de la Huerta on political matters (Moratín defended the king and absolute monarchy while Huerta attacked it), but he did agree with Huerta's conviction that "neither our genius, nor our language, nor our poetry should in any way give in to those of other nations."[2]

Moratín respected foreign literature, but there is nothing French or Italian about him. With the exception of some lip service to French writers — and only then because of their Classical elements — Moratín blithely ignored literary events north of the Pyrenees and even managed to publish various hostile comments about his northern neighbors. His interest in Italy revolved around his friendship with several Italians and, ironically, it was he who encouraged them to carry Spanish literature back to their home ground. He persuaded Conti to translate Garcilaso, and he instructed Signorelli on Spanish drama for the latter's history of drama. Where we might have expected oppressive French and Italian influences upon this most "Pseudoclassical" of authors (if we listen to some critics), we find instead a nearly xenophobic attachment to Spain and a desire to propagate Spanish literature beyond Spain's borders. His own works are intensely nationalistic both in form and content, relying heavily on Renaissance and, perhaps more than he would willingly admit, Golden-Age authors. Lucrecia aside, all of his heroes are Spanish, as are his locales and his preferred themes. We recognize Pelayo, Guzmán, Cortés, Pedro Romero, the Cid, Spanish war heroes, Spanish political figures, and an almost personified Madrid to be his principal characters. He risked becoming exceedingly unpopular by attacking what were regarded as the idols of Spanish literature. He did not adopt foreign ideas but rather integrated certain aspects of what he learned from writers in other countries into his peculiarly Spanish temperament. What comes through in his works is an intense Spanishness, illuminated by a cosmopolitan awareness of the world around him.

If he was a traditionalist in politics, he was far from a conformist in literature. He jeopardized his reputation by going against popular currents and pressures. He chanced the disfavor of his enlightened friends by supporting the bullfight and by exposing and defending prostitution. His most sincere attempts at literary creation were his most honest failures: he wanted his dramas to succeed so they could usher in a new literary mode, a firm entrenchment of that elusive "good taste." But he had rules for everything, and he affixed them to his dramatic writing, his poetic creations, his interpretation of the hunt, and even his "art" of whoring.

Moratín was very young when he wrote his most influential and startling works. He created some of the century's best poetry, most argued-about dramas, most explosive commentaries, and most scandalous verse between the ages of twenty-five and thirty-four. If the prestige enjoyed by people with whom one converses, argues, and drinks is any indication of the importance of that individual, then Moratín basked in the light of reflected glory in the Spain of 1760–80. He counted among his friends kings, queens, princes, ministers, counts, dukes, authors, teachers, musicians, sculptors, economists, and painters. He was sought out, admired, used, attacked, imitated, and befriended by them. He possessed an intriguing personality: like the stereotypical Neoclassicist he could be austere, conservative, moral, and rigid, yet he could be much more. He was passionate, driven, quick, dedicated, talkative, and complex. He was Epicurean and Stoical, and at times Dionysian. In him raged a thesis-antithesis conflict, neither one gaining full control of his mind or activities. At times he was "enlightened," "rational," and responsive to duty; at others he was seduced by the sensual delights and ribald, wild abandon of wine, women, and song.

Neoclassicism and nationalism would join together in Moratín, one of the first eighteenth-century poets to revive the ancient anacreontic ode (as had Villegas, Lope and Quevedo in the century before him) and to develop the color and energy of the traditional Spanish ballad. This was not at all "subconscious,"[3] as one critic

would have it today. Unlike Cadalso, Moratín never traveled
abroad. There is no evidence that, once he arrived back in Madrid
in 1759, he ever left except for short summer visits to the family
dwelling in Pastrana. World culture was brought to him through
books and conversations with his friends, and he shaped that
worldliness to his ardently Spanish orientation. Moratín lived by
his own advice that one should study "Greeks and Spaniards,
Latins and Spaniards, Italians and Spaniards, French and Spaniards, English and Spaniards." For Nicolás Fernández de Moratín
the distinction between Classical and Spanish was a false one: his
Neoclassicism was a very Spanish thing.

Notes and References

Preface

1. Edith Helman, "The Elder Moratín and Goya," *Hispanic Review,* 23 (1955), p. 219.

Chapter One

1. "Testimonio de Nobleza de la familia de Fernández de Moratín," Biblioteca Nacional, 12.168. These documents provide a wealth of genealogical information for the Moratín family, based on marriage and baptismal certificates. Emilio Cotarelo y Mori published several of them in his *Iriarte y su época* (Madrid, 1897), pp. 519–24.

2. Pascual Madoz's *Diccionario geográfico-estadístico-histórico de España y sus posesiones de Ultramar,* 3rd. edition (Madrid, 1848), informs us that Moratín was a "place in the province of Oviedo, town of Salas and parish of Santa Eulalia de Doriga. Located to the right of the Narcea river, on a crest...limey and not too fertile. Products: corn, beans, spelt-wheat, potatoes, and other fruits. Population: 6 families, 28 inhabitants" (volume 11, p. 591). The Testimonio's mentions of Salas and Doriga confirm that this was indeed the family site.

3. Some additional points of interest can be found in a letter written by Leandro in 1782, soliciting a position in the royal household. Archivo General del Palacio, expediente de Nicolás Fernández de Moratín. Reproduced by John C. Dowling, "Moratín, suplicante," *Revista de Archivos, Bibliotecas y Museos,* 68 (1960), p. 502.

4. "Pues no se averguence nadie de conocer la verdad, que así me sucedió a mí, que estaba en el mismo error; porque una tía mía me tenía hecho creer, que no havía cosa más grande, que los Autos." *Desengaño 2,* p. 27.

5. According to testimony of Juan Antonio Melón, recounted by Juan Pérez de Guzmán, "El padre de Moratín," *La España Moderna,* June 1900, p. 17.

6. Miguel became a jeweler and sometime poet (d. 1809); Manuel was sickly and lived supported by his brothers; Ana (d. 1804), who married a jeweler, was Leandro's godmother. See Leandro Fernández de Moratín, "Fragmento de la vida de Moratín," *Obras póstumas de Moratín,* 3

(Madrid, 1867), p. 301; and René Andioc, ed., *Epistolario de Leandro Fernández de Moratín* (Madrid, 1973).

7. Miguel Batllori, *La cultura hispano-italiana de los jesuitas expulsos, 1767-1814* (Madrid, 1966), p. 484.

8. Universidad de Valladolid, *Libro de matrículas de la Facultad de Canones,* Book 73, folio 36 (May 10, 1754); *Libro de la Facultad de Canones,* Book 163, folio 81 (May 11, 1754).

9. Dr. Philip Deacon has completed a dissertation on Moratín which it is hoped will be published without delay. I am grateful to him for sharing some of his observations with me.

10. "Egloga a Velasco y González" (Madrid, 1763), reproduced in the Biblioteca de Autores Españoles (BAE), 2, pp. 22-25.

11. *Ibid.*

12. *Ibid.*

13. "Vida de don Nicolás Fernández de Moratín," originally written for the 1821 edition of his *Obras póstumas* (Barcelona). Reproduced in the 1825 edition (London), and finally in the *Obras de D. Nicolás y D. Leandro Fernández de Moratín,* BAE, 2 (Madrid, 1846). Citation here from p. viii; to be referred to as *Vida.* Unless otherwise indicated, BAE will stand for this volume.

14. BAE, p. 23.

15. Ramón de Mesonero Romanos, *Manual histórico-topográfico, administrativo y artístico de Madrid* (Madrid, 1844), p. 63.

16. The petimetra was a French concept (*petit-maitre*) encompassing in men dandyism or foppishness, and in women snobbery dominated by attention to ostentatious appearance. For a discussion of their types and literary embodiments, see J. Subirá, "Petimetría y majismo en la literatura," *Revista de Literatura,* 4 (1953), pp. 267-85.

17. "Prólogo," *Lucrecia* (Madrid, 1763), p. 7.

18. Julio Mathías, *Moratín: estudio y antología* (Madrid, 1964), p. 213.

19. Francisco Salva Miguel, ed., *Poesía lírica* (Barcelona, 1945), p. xiii.

20. "Prólogo," *El Poeta Matritense* (Madrid, 1764), p. 4. The *Poet* was advertised in the *Diario de Madrid,* January 10, and *Gaceta de Madrid,* February 7, 1764.

21. *Ibid.,* pp. 6-7.

22. Manuel Silvela, "Vida de don Leandro Fernández de Moratín," *Obras póstumas de D. Leandro Fernández de Moratín,* 1 (Madrid, 1867), p. 8.

23. John C. Dowling, *Leandro Fernández de Moratín* (New York, 1971), p. 20.

24. Patricio de la Escosura, "Moratín en su vida íntima," *La Ilustración Española y Americana,* 1 (1877), pp. 305-306.

25. Leandro Fernández de Moratín, "Fragmento," *Op. cit.,* p. 305.

26. "Prólogo," *La Diana* (Madrid, 1765), p. 2.

27. *Ibid.,* pp. 7-8.

28. *La visita del hospital del mundo.* The manuscript copy of the play is

dated 1764 and attributed to Mariana Alcázar, third lady in María Hidalgo's acting company. See Cotarelo y Mori, *D. Ramón de la Cruz y sus obras* (Madrid, 1899), p. 430. Cotarelo believes this manuscript (Biblioteca Municipal, 1-184-39) to be Cruz's.

29. "Egloga a Velasco y González," BAE, p. 23.

30. *El Poeta Matritense,* 9, pp. 147-60; BAE, pp. 25-27. The poem was also printed separately, as an announcement in the *Gaceta de Madrid,* September 16, 1766, indicates. Ayala wrote an elegy as well.

31. "Al Conde de Aranda por los años de 1768 y 1769," in *Obras inéditas de Don Nicolás Fernández de Moratín,* ed. by R. Foulché-Delbosc (Madrid, 1892), pp. 12-18.

32. *Vida,* p. xi.

33. Mesonero Romanos, "Don Nicolás Fernández de Moratín," *Trabajos no coleccionados,* 2 (Madrid, 1903-1905), p. 475.

34. See José Simón Díaz, "Nicolás Fernández de Moratín, opositor a cátedras," *Revista de Filología Española,* 28 (1944), pp. 154-76; José Simón Díaz, *Historia del Colegio Imperial de Madrid,* 2 vols. (Madrid, 1952-59); Russell P. Sebold, "Introducción," to *Numancia destruída* (Salamanca, 1971).

35. Simón Díaz, "Moratín, opositor," p. 160. Simón Díaz publishes both the Latin ode and the Spanish translation.

36. *Vida,* p. xii.

37. *Ibid.*

38. Biblioteca Nacional: manuscript 19.009.

39. The letters have been reproduced by Simón Díaz, "Moratín, opositor," p. 176.

40. See René Andioc, ed., *Diario* (Madrid, 1967), and *Epistolario.*

41. René Andioc, *Teatro y sociedad en el Madrid del siglo XVIII* (Madrid, 1976), p. 468.

42. *Ibid.*

43. See Angel González Palencia, "La Fonda de San Sebastián," *Revista de Archivos, Bibliotecas y Museos,* 2 (1925), pp. 549-53; republished in his *Entre dos siglos* (Madrid, 1943), pp. 117-24.

44. Cadalso, writing from Salamanca in late 1773 or early 1774, reveals that a certain Mr. Dupont, to whom "le escribí dirigida a la fonda de San Sebastián," apparently was in contact with Moratín. René Foulché-Delbosc, "Obras inéditas de Cadalso," *Revue Hispanique,* 1 (1894), p. 305. Glendinning and Dupuis identify him as Juan Dupont in their edition of *Cartas marruecas* (London, 1966), p. 178.

45. This felicitous phrase belongs to Roberto Castrovido, whose "Prólogo" to *Nicolás Fernández de Moratín: Sus mejores versos* (Madrid, 1927), is otherwise taken from the *Vida.*

46. Juan Alborg, *Historia de la literatura española,* 3 (Madrid, 1972), p. 41.

47. Russell P. Sebold, *Cadalso: El primer romántico "europeo" de*

España (Madrid, 1974), p. 227. See Carta 33, Támesis edition.

48. "Al estilo magnífico de don Nicolás Fernández de Moratín en sus composiciones heroicas," BAE, 61, p. 264. A Pindaric ode repeats the sentiments, pp. 264-65.

49. Emilio Cotarelo y Mori, *Iriarte,* p. 136. Published by Foulché-Delbosc, *Obras inéditas de Moratín,* pp. 22-26.

50. BAE, 61, pp. 264-65, 274.

51. In 1725 Juan had published a Latin poem on the subject.

52. See J. Pérez de Guzmán, *op. cit.,* p. 29.

53. See Russell P. Sebold, "Introducción," *Numancia destruida.*

54. John Moore, *Ramón de la Cruz* (New York, 1972), p. 146. See also Vittorio Cian, *Italia e Spagna nel secolo XVIII: Giovambattista Conti e alcune relazioni letterarie fra l'Italia e la Spagna nella seconda metà del settecento* (Torino, 1896).

55. Casimiro Gómez Ortega, "Noticias biográficas de Juan Bautista Conti," Academia de la Historia, Madrid, 9-29-5/5962.

56. Juan Bautista Conti, *La célebre égloga primera de Garcilaso de la Vega* (Madrid, 1771). Announced in the *Gaceta de Madrid,* November 26, 1771.

57. Marcelino Menéndez Pelayo, "Italia y España en el siglo XVIII," *Crítica histórica y literaria,* 4 (Santander, 1942), p. 13.

58. *Obras póstumas* (Barcelona, 1821). See note by Leandro, 1.

59. Menéndez Pelayo, *Ibid.*

60. Juan Sempere y Guarinos, *Ensayo de una biblioteca de los mejores escritores del reinado de Carlos III,* 4 (Madrid, 1969), p. 157.

61. See Aureliano Fernández Guerra, *Lección poética sobre las celebérrimas quintillas de don Nicolás Fernández de Moratín* (Madrid, 1883), p. 9.

62. Foulché-Delbosc, *op. cit.,* p. 308.

63. Elena Catena, "Características generales del siglo XVIII," in J. M. Díez Borque, ed., *Historia de la literatura española (ss. XVII y XVIII* (Madrid, 1975), p. 306.

64. *Vida,* p. xiii.

65. Cotarelo, *Ramón de la Cruz,* p. 150.

66. See César Real de la Riva's classic "La escuela poética salmantina del siglo XVIII," *Boletín de la Biblioteca de Menéndez Pelayo,* 24 (1948), pp. 321-64. Cadalso wrote that "the sonnets [of Moratín] will be read in the academy of Meléndez and his friends who join me in a tertulia for two hours each evening reading our works or others' and subjecting each one of us to the rigid criticism of the other two." Foulché-Delbosc, *op. cit.,* p. 305.

67. Alborg, *Historia,* p. 42; Cotarelo, *Iriarte,* p. 125.

68. John C. Dowling, "The Taurine Works of Nicolás Fernández de Moratín," *South Central Bulletin,* 22, 4 (1962), p. 31.

69. *Desengaño 2,* pp. 19-20.

70. *Vida,* p. xv.

71. *Ibid.,* p. xvi. Cadalso was apparently writing a play on the same theme.

72. He attended over sixty-six weekly or semiweekly meetings between mid-1777 and May 1780, not counting the meetings set aside for special commissions. See the Society's *Actas* and *Libros de Acuerdos.*

73. The *Actas* point out that between October 1777 and February 1780 Moratín conducted growing experiments with the new grain called sulla in his lands in Pastrana, and frequently reported back to the Society on the suitability of the grain and its similarity to other grains.

74. Moratín was less than thorough at times. His approval of the twelve-volume *Memoirs* of Miguel Gerónimo Suárez was two sentences long, one of which suggested that the work was very similar to one written by Juan Cubié. Juan Pío Catalina finds Moratín's judgment unfair: "With all due respect to the indiscutable authority of the illustrious Mr. Moratín, we believe that in judging this work he either did not look at it, or he put in his judgment more cruelty than justice."*Catálogo del Archivo de la Real Sociedad Económica Matritense, 1775–1780* (typescript, 1922), p. 326. For more details see Juan Lesén y Moreno, *Historia de la Sociedad Económica de Amigos de País de Madrid* (Madrid, 1863), pp. 357–58.

75. See Emilio Cotarelo y Mori, *Un gran editor español del siglo XVIII: Biografía de D. Antonio de Sancha* (Madrid, 1924), pp. 60–61.

76. Real Sociedad Económica, Legajo 14, folio 49.

77. Real Sociedad Económica, Legajo 205, folio 18.

78. *Vida,* p. xvii.

79. For example, they both attended the meetings of September 20, September 27, October 4, and October 11. Ayala was assigned to translate some woodworking books into Spanish and to write an ode in honor of Carlos III. *Libro de Acuerdos,* A/110/41.

80. Leandro was also a member later on (as "Inarco Celenio"), as was Vicente García de la Huerta. Antonia Díaz de Lamarque, a forgotten poetess and member of the Arcadians, dedicated verses to a descendant of Nicolás, one Isabel Fernández de Moratín, in 1863. She mentions "Flumisbo" and "Inarco" in the poem. A full study of the Arcadians would add immeasurably to our understanding of eighteenth- and nineteenth-century poetic activity.

81. Juan Álvarez y Baena, *Hijos de Madrid,* 4 (Madrid, 1791), p. 143.

82. *Desengaño* 1, p. 8.

83. *El arte de las putas.* Ed. by Manuel Fernández Nieto (Madrid, 1977), p. 124.

84. *Vida,* p. xviii.

85. Real Sociedad Económica, Legajo 14, folio 49.

86. *Gaceta de Madrid* made the Academy's announcement on July 9, 1779, still not knowing the author's identity, which was finally revealed in the issue of July 27.

87. Manuel Silvela, *op. cit.,* pp. 9–11. Silvela dramatizes the situation by adding a suspenseful dialogue between the father, announcing the Academy's honorable mention to an unknown, and Leandro, trembling as he reveals himself to be that author.

88. *Diario,* Biblioteca Nacional, Manuscript 5617. This is the first part of what has become known as Leandro's diary; Nicolás's entries run from January 1778 to May 1780.

89. See Fernando Díaz Plaja, *La vida española en el siglo XVIII* (Barcelona, 1946), p. 93. Juan Pérez de Guzmán, *op. cit.,* pp. 29–31, details some of the books which Moratín was charged with reviewing. One of them was Iriarte's translation of Horace's *Poetics.*

90. *Vida,* p. xix.

91. *Diario.* Joaquín de Entrambasaguas mistakenly writes that Nicolás died in the house on Fomento St.: *El Madrid de Moratín* (Madrid, 1960), p. 17. That he died in the Cava Baja is confirmed in his death certificate.

92. Archivo Histórico Nacional, Legajo 7306.

93. Dowling, "Moratín, suplicante," p. 302.

94. See for example René Andioc's introduction to Leandro's diary (Madrid, 1967), p. 16.

95. BAE, p. 558.

96. The actor was the fiftyish Manuel de Inca Yupanqui; Nicolás had given him acting lessons as well.

97. Juan Nicasio Gallego, "Examen del Juicio Crítico...de José Hermosilla," BAE, 67, p. 432.

98. René Andioc, *Teatro y sociedad,* p. 504.

99. José Martínez Ruiz ("Azorín"), "Moratín," *Obras completas,* 1 (Madrid, 1959), p. 53. Originally published in 1893.

Chapter Two

1. Russell P. Sebold, "A Statistical Analysis of the Origins and Nature of Luzán's Ideas on Poetry," *Hispanic Review,* 35 (1967), pp. 227–51. Moratín cites Luzán several times in *Reproach 2.*

2. The title pages carry no dates or numbers; Cotarelo convincingly dates them November 1762, September 1763, and October 1763. They were unfortunately left out, along with Moratín's prologues, of Leandro's editions of the *Posthumous Works* and of the BAE edition. Hartzenbusch published selections of 1 and 2 in his BAE 7.

3. *Reproach 1,* p. 2.

4. *Ibid.,* p. 3.

5. *Ibid.,* p. 5.

6. *Ibid.*

7. *Ibid.,* p. 8.

8. For a discussion of what was transpiring in Seville, see Francisco Aguilar Piñal, *Sevilla y el teatro en el siglo XVIII* (Oviedo, 1974).

9. This is a play on Lope's treatise *El arte nuevo de hacer comedias.*

10. *Reproach 1*, p. 10.

11. *Ibid.*, p. 12.

12. *Ibid.*, p. 16.

13. *Ibid.*, p. 11

14. *Belianís Literario*, 3, pp. 78–79.

15. *Reproach 2*, pp. 18–19.

16. *Ibid.*, p. 19.

17. *Ibid.*, pp. 20–21. He repeats the idea in *Reproach 3*, p. 46.

18. *Ibid.*, pp. 22–23. Surprisingly, Moratín's closed-mindedness about the appropriateness of allegory in the *autos* is still being echoed. Alborg finds it "certain that in the *autos* it is carried to an extreme. . . ." *Historia*, p. 588.

19. *Ibid.*, p. 23.

20. Cited by Fernando Lázaro Carreter, "Ignacio de Luzán y el Neoclasicismo," *Universidad*, 37 (1960), p. 65.

21. *Reproach 2*, p. 27.

22. *Ibid.*, p. 29.

23. *Ibid.*, p. 37.

24. "To say that the *autos* receive common applause is an obvious lie; because intelligent people abhor them for their deformities, and idiots do not understand them" *Reproach 2*, p. 35.

25. *Ibid.*, p. 37.

26. *Ibid.*, p. 39.

27. Details of the polemic can be found in Andioc, *Teatro y sociedad;* Cotarelo, *Bibliografía de las controversias sobre la licitud del teatro en España* (Madrid, 1904); I. L. McClelland, *The Origins of the Romantic Movement in Spain* (Liverpool, 1937); and Menéndez Pelayo, *Historia de las ideas estéticas en España*, 3 (Santander, 1940). Some of the flurry of papers involved are: *La comedia española, defendida*, by D. Luis Jayme (alias); *La pensadora gaditana*, by Doña Beatriz Cienfuegos; *El escritor sin título*, by D. J. C. Romea y Tapia; the anonymous *Belianís Literario;* and others. All notices are taken from the *Gaceta de Madrid* and the *Diario de Madrid.*

28. Cristóbal Romea y Tapia, *El escritor sin título*, 1763, pp. 59–60. The Sixth Discourse encompasses pp. 183–226.

29. *Reproach 3*, p. 41.

30. *Ibid.*, p. 43.

31. The copy I have reads "inverosimil," an obvious misprint, p. 43.

32. *Ibid.*, pp. 73–78.

33. For an excellent discussion of these matters see A. A. Parker, *The Allegorical Dramas of Calderón* (London, 1943), and Marcel Bataillon, "Ensayo de explicación del 'auto sacramental,' " in *Varia lección de clásicos españoles* (Madrid, 1964), pp. 183–205. Documentation may be found in Ramón Esquer Torres, "Las prohibiciones de comedias y autos sacramentales en el siglo XVIII," *Segismundo*, 1, ii (1965), pp. 187–226.

Clavijo's intervention is discussed by Agustín Espinosa, *Don José Clavijo y Fajardo* (Gran Canaria, 1970).

34. The *Gaceta de Madrid* announced the volumes in February and April 1760. Moratín may have consulted this edition.

35. Review of the *Obras póstumas* (1825) in *Foreign Review,* 1 (1828), pp. 415-29. Quote here is from pp. 416-17.

36. Roberto Castrovido, *op. cit.,* p. 13.

37. Joaquín de Entrambasaguas, "El teatro en el siglo XVIII," in J. M. Díez Borque, ed., *Historia de la literatura española (siglos XVIII y XVIII)* (Madrid, 1975), p. 254. The "only lasting work" quote is taken directly from Mesonero.

38. Alborg, p. 588.

39. Andioc sees religion in the same light. *Teatro y sociedad,* p. 371.

40. "A la Excma. Señora Doña Mariana de Silva y Toledo, Duquesa de la Ciudad de Medinasidonia...," with *La petimetra,* p. 3. Hartzenbusch republished the prologue in BAE, 7, pp. lxvi-lxix.

41. *Ibid.,* "Dissertation," p. 4.

42. *Ibid.*

43. *Ibid.,* pp. 19-20. J. Cook sees Moratín's praise of Lope and Calderón as false" "...he succeeded in fooling no one. His real views at that time were too well known." *Neoclassic Drama in Spain* (Dallas, 1959), p. 211. Ms. McClelland claims that his praise was "for the purpose of ingratiating himself with the public," *Origins,* p. 88. But this was not so; his admiration for certain aspects of Golden-Age plays was very real.

44. *Ibid.,* p. 6.

45. *Ibid.,* p. 9.

46. *Ibid.,* p. 10.

47. *Ibid.,* p. 11. Cook recognized Moratín's debt to Luzán, *op. cit.,* p. 210.

48. *Ibid.,* p. 16.

49. *Ibid.,* p. 21.

50. "Prólogo" to *Lucrecia* (Madrid, 1763), pp. 3-4.

51. *Ibid.,* pp. 5-6.

52. *Ibid.,* p. 7.

53. *Vida,* p. viii.

54. B. Jarnés, *Enciclopedia de la literatura,* 2 (Mexico, n.d.), p. 648.

55. J. Arce, "Diversidad temática y lingüística en la lírica dieciochesca," *Cuadernos de la Cátedra Feijoo,* 22 (1970), p. 33.

56. "Prólogo" to *El Poeta Matritense* (Madrid, 1764), 6.

57. Satire 1. *El Poeta Matritense,* 3, p. 42. Reproduced in BAE, pp. 31-32. I shall cite from the BAE edition which is more accessible and in the case of these satires, completely faithful to the original edition.

58. See Quevedo's "Epístola satírica y censoria contra las costumbres presentes de los castellanos, escrita a don Gaspar de Guzmán, Conde de Olivares, en su valimiento."

59. Sadly, Moratín's contribution is still being misinterpreted: "Moratín was one of the most implacable enemies of the Spanish Golden Age theater. *By his decree* the performance of the *autos sacramentales* was prohibited..." F. C. Sainz de Robles, *Ensayo de un diccionario de la literatura,* 2 (Madrid, 1964), p. 391. Emphasis added.

Chapter Three

1. See Joaquín Arce, "La poesía en el siglo XVIII," in J. M. Díez Borque, ed., *Historia de la literatura española,* p. 374.

2. Leandro states that his father met María Ladvenant "a few months" after arriving in Madrid in late 1759. It is likely that he met her sister at the same time or shortly thereafter. *Vida,* p. viii. For additional documents see E. Julia Martínez, "Documentos sobre María y Francisca Ladvenant," *Boletín de la Real Academia Española,* 1 (1914), pp. 468-69.

3. Cotarelo, *Don Ramón de la Cruz* (Madrid, 1899), pp. 535-36; *María Ladvenant y Quirante* (Madrid, 1896), pp. 41-43; *Iriarte,* pp. 96-97.

4. Leandro's diary reveals the extent of his amorous adventures. See José Luis Cano, "Moratín en su *Diario,"* *Heterodoxos y prerrománticos* (Madrid, 1974), pp. 23-28. For a different view, see Russell P. Sebold's review of the diary in *Hispanic Review,* 39 (1971), 106-10.

5. The only poems which Aribau failed to pick up were an epigram, "A un hombrón," that originally appeared in the *Poet,* 5, four verses to Garcilaso published by Conti in 1771, and the later ones discovered by Foulché.

6. I will give references to the poems both from the original *Poet* and from the BAE edition, since their arrangements differ.

7. Horace: *Poet,* 7; BAE, p. 35. Pindar: *Poet,* 5; BAE, p. 38. Marcial: *Poet,* 5; BAE, p. 15. See also Menéndez Pelayo, *Horacio en España,* 2 (Madrid, 1885), pp. 113-15.

8. Biblioteca Nacional: Manuscript 19.009.

9. J. Soubeyroux, "Des bienfaits de la corrida en Espagne au XVIIIe siècle," *Bulletin Hispanique,* 76 (1974), pp. 183-91.

10. See J. M. Cossío's *Los toros* (Madrid, 1943). Also John C. Dowling, "The Taurine Works of Nicolás Fernández de Moratín," *South Central Bulletin,* 22 (1962), pp. 31-34.

11. "A Pedro Romero, torero insigne," BAE, p. 37.

12. Madrid: Pantaleón Aznar, 1777. Reprinted in Madrid in 1801, Valencia in 1815, and in the BAE, pp. 141-44.

13. See Enrique Lafuente Ferrari, "Ilustración y elaboración en la 'Tauromaquia' de Goya," *Archivo Español de Arte,* 75 (1946), pp. 177-216; Gaspar Gómez de la Serna, "Goya y los toros," *La Estafeta Literaria,* 484 (1972), pp. 4-9 and 485 (1972), pp. 12-16.

14. Letter to Mélon, August 28, 1823. Andioc, *Epistolario,* p. 563.

15. José Escobar, *Los orígines de la obra de Larra* (Madrid, 1973), pp. 176–81.

16. Leandro Fernández de Moratín, "Fragmento," *Obras póstumas,* 3 (Madrid, 1867), p. 303.

17. J. M. Cossío, "La fiesta de toros en Madrid. Oda a Pedro Romero," *Boletín de la Biblioteca Menéndez Pelayo,* 8 (1926), p. 234.

18. Dowling, "Taurine Works," p. 32.

19. Aureliano Fernández Guerra, *Lección poética.*

20. F. Lázaro Carreter, "La transmisión textual de 'fiesta de toros en Madrid,'" *Clavileño,* 4, 21 (1953), pp. 33–38.

21. Alborg, *Historia,* p. 398.

22. Both versions appear in Fernández Guerra, *Lección poética.*

23. Castrovido, "Prólogo," p. 15.

24. Fernández Guerra, *op. cit.*

25. N. Alonso Cortés, "Sobre la 'Fiesta de toros en Madrid'," *Artículos histórico-literarios* (Valladolid, 1935), pp. 5–11.

26. McClelland, *Origins,* p. 298.

27. Cossío, "La fiesta de toros," p. 234.

28. E. A. Peers, *A History of the Romantic Movement in Spain,* 1 (Cambridge, 1940), p. 18.

29. M. Menéndez Pelayo, *Historia de las ideas estéticas en España,* 5 (Santander, 1940), p. 284.

30. J. H. Mundy, "Some Aspects of the Poetry of Juan Artolas," *Liverpool Studies in Spanish Literature* (Liverpool, 1940), pp. 144–74.

31. P. Viñolas, *Episodio lírico para representar en el teatro* (Barcelona, 1870).

32. Cossío provides numerous convincing examples in *Los toros en la poesía castellana,* 1 (Madrid, 1931).

33. F. Lázaro Carreter, "La poesía lírica en España durante el siglo XVIII," in G. Díaz Plaja, ed., *Historia general de las literaturas hispánicas,* 4, 1 (Barcelona, 1968), p. 55.

34. Phalaris: a tyrant (570–54 B.C.) known for his cruelty; he imprisoned his enemies and roasted them alive in a hollow brass bull.

35. "Historical Letter," BAE, p. 143.

36. Cossío, *Los toros en la poesía,* 1, 219 ss.

37. Moratín makes reference to the "brave bulls" in the "Eclogue to Velasco and González," 1763.

38. See I. Luzán's "Juicio de París renovado entre el Poder, el Ingenio y el Amor," BAE, 61, pp. 111–15.

39. *El arte de las putas,* ed. Manuel Fernández Nieto, p. 116. Cándido is discussed in the "Historical Letter."

40. Tomás de Iriarte, "Vejamen que hizo D. Thomas de Iriarte, Archivero de la Secretaria del estado, al Idilio, que dio a la imprenta D. Nicolás Fernández de Moratín, Socio de la Sociedad Matritense,"

Biblioteca Nacional: manuscript 10951, folios 61-72. Published by Cotarelo, *Iriarte,* pp. 496-503.

41. *Indice de los libros prohibidos y mandados expurgar* (Madrid, 1790), p. 16.

42. *El arte de las putas* (Madrid, 1898). José Caso González speculates that the editor was Cotarelo. I am grateful to Da. María Brey de Rodríguez-Moñino, who very generously permitted me to study the manuscript and who gave me a photocopy of the first printed edition.

43. M. Menéndez Pelayo, *Historia de los heterodoxos españoles,* 5 (Santander, 1947), p. 304.

44. See note 39 above. I will cite by page number as the verses are miscounted in several places. The other edition is by A. Popof (Mexico, 1978).

45. The reference to Liarta is made in the entry of June 5, 1780 (less than one month after Nicolás's death). *Diario,* p. 24. Andioc writes: "Could it be the prostitute Liarta 'who is still a young girl' in the era when D. Nicolás writes his *Whores' Art?"*

46. Jovellanos, Satire 2, vv. 136-38. See J. Caso González and G. Demerson, "La Sátira de Jovellanos sobre la mala educación de la nobleza," *Revue Hispanique,* 61 (1959), pp. 365-85.

47. I have dealt with autobiographical details at greater length in " 'El cantor de las doncellas' y las rameras madrileñas: Nicolás Fernández de Moratín en el *Arte de las putas,"* *Actas del 6° Congreso Internacional de Hispanistas* (Toronto, in press).

48. See Edith Helman's excellent study.

49. For a development of this theme in Horozco, see A. J. Farrell, "Sebastián de Horozco and the Poetic Tradition of the Cofradía del grillimón'," to appear in *Hispanófila;* also Jack Weiner, "El 'Santo Grillimón' en un poema del *Cancionero* de Sebastián de Horozco," *Hispanófila,* 49 (1973), pp. 11-16.

50. See Bruno Damiani, *Francisco Delicado* (New York, 1974), pp. 103-109.

51. Xavier Domingo, *Erótica hispánica* (Paris, 1972), p. 157. See also José Deleito y Piñuela, *La mala vida en la España de Felipe IV* (Madrid, 1967).

52. "...compared defect by defect, [Moratín's] is vastly superior to the one selected by the Academy." José Vargas Ponce, *Declamación contra los abusos introducidos en el castellano* (Madrid, 1793), p. xxii.

53. *Las naves de Cortés destruidas. Canto épico. Obra posthuma. Ilustrada por el editor con varias reflexiones críticas para la instrucción de la juventud* (Madrid, 1785). Announced in the *Memorial Literario* in November.

54. Dowling's three articles on the subject are: "A Poet Rewrites History: Nicolás Fernández de Moratín and the Burning of Cortés's Ships," *South Atlantic Bulletin,* 41 (1976), pp. 66-73; "Tres versiones de *Las*

naves de Cortés destruidas de Nicolás Fernández de Moratín," to appear in *Homenaje a Agapito Rey* (Indiana University); and "El texto primitivo de *Las naves de Cortés destruidas* de Nicolás Fernández de Moratín," *Boletín de la Real Academia Española,* 57 (1977), pp. 431–83. I am extremely grateful to Professor Dowling for his generosity in providing me with typescripts of these last two articles. Strophe numbers correspond to the manuscript version.

55. Juan Antonio Loche has been suggested as the author of the "Critical Reflections" which were added to the 1785 edition. We do not know whether he or Leandro was responsible for the commentary and the changes, but given Leandro's persistent hand in rewriting his father's works, it is not difficult to favor Leandro as the author of the poem's changes. The prologue and critical reflections are another matter, and it is impossible to establish conclusively their authorship. Certainly, as Andioc has shown, it was Loche who petitioned for and received official permission to publish the work. Archivo Histórico Nacional: Consejos, Impresiones, 5550, n. 2 (See Andioc, *Epistolario,* 150).

56. *Eco de Comerico,* May 12, 1834.

57. *Gaceta de Madrid,* October 10, 1777. Reproduced by Dowling, "Texto primitivo," p. 433–35.

58. See Signorelli's letter to Leandro, January 3, 1786. Published by C. G. Mininni, *Pietro Napoli Signorelli* (Castello, 1914), pp. 343–44.

59. "Prólogo," *Las naves de Cortés destruidas,* 1785, p. 6.

60. Alcalá: Pedro López, 1787. Included in his *Obras completas,* 2 (Madrid, 1792), pp. 207–68.

61. Dowling, "Texto primitivo," p. 443.

62. "Eclogue to Velasco and González," BAE, p. 24.

63. "Al piadoso Augusto y Católico Monarca Carlos III," n.p., n.d.

64. "Egloga a Velasco y González, famosos españoles, con motivo de haverse hecho sus Efigies en la Real Academia de San Fernando, por mando del Rey nuestro Señor" (Madrid, 1763). The competition was announced in the *Gaceta* on February 1, 1763; Moratín's completed poem was advertised in the *Diario de Madrid,* July 19, and in the *Gaceta,* August 23, 1763.

65. *Diana o el arte de la caza* (Madrid, 1765). Announced in the *Gaceta,* September 24. See the interesting article by J. Arce, "Idolos científicos en la poesía española de la Ilustración," *Cuadernos Hispano-Americanos,* 322–23 (1977), pp. 78–96.

66. Sempere, *Biblioteca,* 4, p. 124.

67. "Idilio" (Madrid, 1777), reprinted in the *Memorias de la Sociedad Económica,* 2 (Madrid, 1780); "Egloga," (Madrid, 1778), reprinted in the *Memorias de la Sociedad Económica,* 3 Madrid, 1787); "Elegía" (Madrid, 1779).

68. "Reconvención amistosa al autor del Vejamen contra Moratín." Biblioteca Nacional: Manuscript 19.009. Cotarelo published selections

from Moratín's "A D. Tomás de Iriarte, por su libro contra el colector del *Parnaso*. Epístola," *Iriarte*, pp. 178–79.

69. Letter written on December 7, 1778. Biblioteca Nacional: Manuscript 3172 (papeles de Iriarte).

70. Details of Moratín's activities can be found in the Society's *Legajos* and *Libros de Acuerdos*.

71. N. Glendinning, *A Literary History of Spain. The Eighteenth Century* (New York, 1972), p. 72.

72. Letter published by R. Foulché-Delbosc, "Obras inéditas de Cadalso," *Revue Hispanique*, 1 (1894), p. 305.

73. McClelland, *Origins*, p. 291.

Chapter Four

1. Leandro Fernández de Moratín, "Discurso preliminar," to *Comedias*, BAE, 2, p. 316.

2. Cotarelo, *Iriarte*, p. 43.

3. José Joaquín de Mora, Review of Moratín's *Obras póstumas. Crónica Política y Literaria* (Buenos Aires), August 7, 1827. I am indebted to Professor Luis Monguió for his generosity in sending me this review.

4. Julio Cejador y Frauca, *Historia de la lengua y literatura castellana*, 6 (Madrid, 1917), p. 156.

5. J. Pérez de Guzmán, *op. cit.*, p. 25.

6. Alberto Lista. Cited by E. A. Peers, *op. cit.*, p. 184.

7. Leandro Fernández de Moratín, "Discurso preliminar," *ibid.*

8. Nicolás informs us that a friend in Cádiz tried unsuccessfully to have it staged. *Reproach 1*, p. 8. Announcements of the printed version appeared in the *Gaceta* (July 6, 1762; August 22, 1763) and in the *Diario* (July 7, 1762; November 25, 1762). A careful inspection of the newspapers of the period reveals the paucity of new plays being offered.

9. BAE, p. 84. With the exception of minor punctuation, the BAE edition of Moratín's four plays is faithful to the first editions. All references will be to the BAE edition and page numbers and Act/Scene references will be included in the text.

10. José Caso González offers an interesting interpretation of the play as a Rococo piece in his article "rococó, prerromanticismo y neoclasicismo en el teatro español del siglo XVIII," *Cuadernos de la Cátedra Feijoo*, 22 (1970), pp. 7–29. Caso very astutely recognizes the drama's Spanish roots.

11. See J. H. R. Polt, ed., *Poesía española del siglo XVIII* (Madrid, 1975), pp. 67, 227.

12. Moratín's "Dissertation," pp. 13–14.

13. *El sí de las niñas*, Act 3, Scene 2.

14. "Dissertation," pp. 21-22.

15. J. E. Hartzenbusch, ed., *Comedias de Calderón*. BAE, 7, p. 1.

16. "This work, printed in 1762, lacks comic force, propriety and correct style; and by mixing the defects of our old comedies with the forced regularity to which the author tried to reduce it, there resulted an imitation of an ambiguous nature and little fit to sustain itself in the theater" ("Discurso preliminar," p. 316).

17. *Storia critica d'teatri antichi e moderni*, 6, (Naples, 1790), pp. 67-70. Cited by Cotarelo, *Iriarte*, p. 43.

18. Cited by Leandro, *Vida*, p. xvi.

19. Announcements appeared in the *Diario* on June 10, and in the *Gaceta* on June 10 and August 23; it was still being sold as late as 1782.

20. *Vida*, p. viii.

21. *Ibid.*

22. Moratín claims his sources to be Titus Livy, Valerius Maximus, Florus, and Dionysius, but La Barrara points out that he does not strictly adhere to their accounts. *Aduana crítica*, p. 118. Ramond R. MacCurdy discusses wide uses of the Lucretia theme (more than fifty of Lope's plays contain allusions to her) in his "The Uses of the Rape of Lucretia," *Estudios literarios de hispanistas norteamericanos dedicados u Helmut Hatzfeld* (Barcelona, 1974), pp. 297-308. See also J. Gillet, "Lucrecianecia," *Hispanic Review*, 15 (1947), pp. 120-36.

23. René Andioc thinks differently. "El teatro en el siglo XVIII," in Díez Borque, *op. cit.*, p. 446.

24. Joaquín José Flores? I have been unable to locate this critique of *Lucrecia*, alluded to by Juan Sempere, *Ensayo*, 4, p. 121, and by Alvarez y Baena, *op. cit.*, p. 143. Did Flores write the critique attributed to La Barrera?

25. See, for example, F. Martínez de la Rosa's comment that *Hormesinda* was "the first original tragedy of any merit that appeared at that time." "Apéndice sobre la tragedia española," *Obras*, 3 (Madrid, 1962), p. 149. I. L. McClelland makes some interesting observations on *Hormesinda* in her *Spanish Drama of Pathos 1750-1808*, 1 (Toronto, 1970), pp. 145-64.

26. Ignacio Bernascone, "Prólogo," *Hormesinda* (Madrid, 1770), p. 18.

27. *El Pelayo: Poema Heroyco*, first advertised in the *Diario* (then called the *Diario Noticioso Universal)* on November 26, 1760. It was announced again on February 13, 1762.

28. *Vida*, p. xi.

29. Archivo Municipal de Madrid, Sección de Espectáculos, Legajo I-351-2. Cited by Cotarelo, *Iriarte*, 84n. See C. B. Qualia, "The Campaign to Substitute French Neo-Classical Tragedy for the Comedia, 1762-1800," *Publications of the Modern Language Association*, 54 (1939), p. 209.

30. The plays were *La puente de Mantible, El médico de su honra,* and *El alcalde de Zalamea.* Andioc, *Teatro y sociedad,* p. 23.

31. Valuable information on the actors who played the various roles in *Hormesinda* can be found in Cotarelo's *Ramón de la Cruz.*

32. See D. H. Pageaux's discussion of the Pelayo plays in "Le thème de la résistence asturienne dans la tragedie néo-classique espagnole," *Mélange à la mémoire de Jean Sarrailh,* 2 (Paris, 1966), pp. 235–42. Jovellanos wrote his *Pelayo* in 1769, before the appearance of Moratín's play, but he did make changes in it in 1771 and 1772. "Prólogo," to *Pelayo,* BAE, 46, p. 51. A. Dérozier compares *Hormesinda* to Quintana's Pelayo in *M. J. Quintana et la naissance du libéralisme en Espagne,* 1 (Paris, 1968), pp. 103–105.

33. Biruté Ciplijauskaite, "Lo nacional en el siglo XVIII español," *Archivum,* 22 (1972), p. 106.

34. Juan Peláez, *Reparos sobre la tragedia intitulada Hormesinda, y contra su Prólogo* (Madrid, 1770), p. 51.

35. Bernascone, *op. cit.,* p. 1.

36. *Ibid.,* p. 3.

37. Peláez, *op. cit.,* p. 8.

38. Letter published by Cotarelo, *Iriarte,* pp. 433–47.

39. Cited by McClelland, *Spanish Drama,* 1, pp. 151–52.

40. Cotarelo, *Iriarte,* p. 435.

41. *Ibid.,* p. 447.

42. It was never produced; the printed version was announced on November 4, 1777, in the *Gaceta* and as late as May 1, 1801, in the *Diario,* but copies became difficult to find. Leandro had to write to Juan Melón from Barcelona to request a copy as he was preparing the edition of his father's works. Letter dated November 21, 1820. See *Epistolario,* p. 419.

43. *Vida,* pp. xvi–xvii.

44. "Empresa de Micer Jaques Borgoñon," BAE, pp. 10–12.

45. Prologue to *Guzmán el Bueno* (Madrid, 1777), p. 7.

46. *Ibid.,* p. 10.

47. *Ibid.,* p. 11.

48. Sempere, *Ensayo,* 4, p. 125.

49. Andioc, *Teatro y sociedad,* p. 388.

50. *Vida,* p. xvii.

51. See the examples developed by A. A. Parker in *The Approach to the Spanish Drama of the Golden Age* (London, 1957).

52. Manuscript, New York Public Library. I am grateful to Dr. Deacon for bringing this to my attention.

53. Prologue to *Guzmán el Bueno,* p. 9.

54. *Ibid.,* p. 11.

55. McClelland, *Spanish Drama,* 1, p. 151.

56. Juan Sempere y Guarinos, "Discurso sobre el gusto actual de los

españoles en la literatura," in *Reflexiones sobre el buen gusto* (Madrid, 1782), p. 237.

57. *Aduana crítica,* p. 101.

58. Julio Mathias, *Moratín. Estudio y antología* (Madrid, 1964), p. 214; Agustín del Saz, "La tragedia y comedia neoclásicas," in G. Díaz Plaja, *op. cit.,* p. 132.

59. Angel Valbuena Prat, *Historia del teatro español* (Barcelona, 1956), p. 453.

Chapter Five

1. Cited by Andioc, *Teatro y sociedad,* p. 143.
2. *Ibid.,* p. 299.
3. Valbuena Prat, *op. cit.,* p. 462.

Selected Bibliography

PRIMARY SOURCES

1. General Collections

El Poeta Matritense. Madrid: Miguel Escribano, 1764–66.

Obras póstumas. Madrid: Viuda de Roca, 1821.

Obras póstumas. London: M. Calero, 1825. Reprint of 1821 edition.

Poesías escogidas de Nicolás y Leandro Fernández de Moratín. Valencia: S. Ferrer de Orga, 1830.

Obras de don Nicolás y don Leandro Fernández de Moratín. Edited by B. Carlos Aribau. Biblioteca de Autores Españoles, 2. Madrid: Rivadeneyra, 1846.

Poesías de Moratín padre e hijo. Madrid, 1874. All previously printed in BAE.

Poesías sueltas y obras en prosa [of Leandro], *seguidas de las obras poéticas y dramáticas de Don Nicolás Fernández de Moratín.* Paris: Garnier, 1882. All previously printed in BAE.

Poesías inéditas. Edited by René Foulché-Delbosc. Madrid: Murillo, 1892. Contains five poems not collected elsewhere.

Sus mejores versos. Edited with a prologue by Roberto Castrovido. Madrid: Colegio de Sordomudos y Ciegos, 1927. All previously printed in BAE.

Poesía lírica. Edited by F. Salva Miguel. Barcelona: Montaner y Simón, 1945. All previously printed in BAE.

2. Drama

La petimetra. Comedia nueva. Madrid: Viuda de Juan Muñoz, 1762. First edition.

Lucrecia. Tragedia. Madrid: Joseph Francisco Martínez Abad, 1763. First edition.

Hormesinda. Tragedia. Madrid: Pantaleón Aznar, 1770. First edition. Contains a prologue by I. Bernascone plus poems by J. Iriarte, J. B. Conti, and C. Gómez Ortega.

Hormesinda. Second edition. Barcelona: Carlos Gilbert, n.d. (Listed as "corregida y enmendada" but it is same as first edition.)

La defensa de Melilla. 1775. Comedy mentioned by Leandro; lost.

El ridículo don Sancho. Comedy mentioned by Signorelli; lost.

Guzmán el Bueno. Tragedia. Madrid: Antonio de Sancha, 1777. First edition. Contains prologue by Moratín.

173

Guzmán the Brave or the First Siege of Gibraltar. New York Public Library, manuscript. Play altered in translation, 1802.

3. Prose

Desengaño al teatro español, respuesta al romance liso y llano y defensa del Pensador. Madrid, 1762? *Desengaño 1.*

Desengaño al teatro español, sobre los autos sacramentales de don Pedro Calderón de la Barca. Madrid, 1763? *Desengaño 2.*

Desengaño al teatro español, sobre los autos sacramentales de don Pedro Calderón de la Barca. Madrid, 1763? *Desengaño 3.*

Reflexiones críticas dirigidas al colector de el Parnaso, Juan López Sedano. Written with Ignacio López de Ayala. Mentioned by Leandro; unpublished; lost.

Examen tardío pero cierto de algunas piezas del teatro, en especial de la zarzuela intitulada El buen marido y nota que hay al fin de ella. Cotarelo says, "razonablemente habrá que atribuir a Moratín." Lost?

Extracto de la Memoria del Sr. D. Nicolás Fernández de Moratín, in *Memorias de la Sociedad Económica,* 1 (Madrid: Sancha, 1780), 322–33. Parts of his treatise on agricultural production.

"Carta histórica sobre el origen y progresos de las fiestas de toros en España," Madrid: Pantaléon Aznar, 1777. Reprinted in Madrid (Repullés, 1801) and Valencia (Monfort, 1815).

Diario. Biblioteca Nacional: Manuscript 5617. January 1778–May 1780.

4. Poetry (Poems published separately and/or not included in BAE)

"Al piadoso Augusto y Católico Monarca Don Carlos III por el perdón concedido a los Reos el día veinte de Septiembre de este año de mil setecientos sesenta y dos." N.p., n d. First published poem.

"Egloga a Velasco y González." Madrid: Miguel Escribano, 1763. Written for a celebration of the Royal Academy of San Fernando.

La Diana o el arte de la caza. Madrid: Miguel Escribano, 1765. Didactic poem in six Cantos.

"Amor, tú que a mi verso," ode. In J. B. Conti, *La célebre égloga primera de Garcilaso.* Madrid: Ibarra, 1771. Not in BAE.

"Hermosas ninfas, que entre juncia," sonnet. In Conti, *op. cit.* Not in BAE.

"Las verdes Drias del undoso río," sonnet. In Conti, *op cit.* Not in BAE.

"¿Ves con la acorde musa?," ode with Latin translation. In Conti, *op. cit.* Not in BAE.

"La fiesta de toros en Madrid." Biblioteca Nacional: Manuscript 19.009. Reprinted in Manuel José Quintana, *Poesías selectas castellanas,* 4. Madrid, 1830.

"Idilio" to the students of the Real Sociedad Económica. Madrid: Ibarra, 1777. Different from BAE version. Reprinted in the *Memorias de la Sociedad Económica, 2.* Madrid: Sancha, 1787.

"Las naves de Cortés destruidas." Real Academia Española, 1778. Manuscript. Published first in a different form in 1785. Madrid: Imprenta Real. Included in J. M. Quintana, *Poesías selectas castellanas,* 3. Madrid: Gómez Fuentenebro, 1807; Quintana, *Tesoro del Parnaso Español,* 4. Perpiñán: J. A. Alzine, 1817; Quintana, *Poesías selectas castellanas,* 4. Madrid, 1830; BAE; and BAE, 29.

"Egloga" to the students of the Real Sociedad Económica. Madrid: Ibarra, 1778. Omitted from BAE. Reprinted in *Memorias de la Sociedad Económica,* 3. Madrid: Sancha, 1787.

"Elegía" to the students of the Real Sociedad Económica. Madrid: Ibarra, 1779. Loaded with historical and topographical information on Madrid.

El arte de las putas. Madrid, 1898. First published edition. Republished by Manuel Fernández Nieto. Madrid: Siro, 1977. Another edition by A. Popof. Mexico: Premia Editora, 1978.

"Al descubrimiento de Herculano," ode with Latin translation. In José Simón Díaz, "Nicolás Fernández de Moratín, opositor a cátedras." *Revista de Filología Española,* 28 (1944), 157-60. Poems written for the Imperial College oppositions in 1770. Not in BAE.

"Donde junto al Averno entre altas hayas," tercets. In Simón Díaz, "Moratín, opositor," 161-62. For the 1770 Imperial College oppositions. Not in BAE.

"A quien tu Melpomene una vez sola," translation of Horace, Book 4, Ode 3. Biblioteca Nacional: Manuscript 3745. Unpublished.

"Canción pindárica . . . con motivo de los primeros actos públicos de poética en los Reales Estudios de Madrid." Biblioteca Nacional: Manuscript 19.009. Unpublished.

"O Nave volverate al mar hinchado," translation of Horace, Book 1, Ode 14. Biblioteca Nacional: Manuscript 3745. Unpublished.

"Reconvención amistosa al autor del Vejamen contra Moratín," ballad. Biblioteca National: Manuscript 19.009. Unpublished.

SECONDARY SOURCES

ALBORG, JUAN LUIS. *Historia de la literatura española: siglo XVIII.* Madrid: Gredos, 1972. At times nasty, but a valuable study.

ALONSO CORTÉS, NARCISO. "Sobre la 'Fiesta de toros en Madrid,'" *Artículos histórico-literarios* (Valladolid: Imprenta Castellana, 1935), 5-11. Study of sources, finding similarities with popular literature of the past.

ALVAREZ Y BAENA, JOSÉ ANTONIO. "Nicolás Fernández de Moratín." *Hijos de Madrid,* 4 (1791), 142-44. Near-contemporary biographical information.

ANDIOC, RENÉ, ed. *Epistolario de Leandro Fernández de Moratín.* Madrid: Castalia, 1973. Many references to Nicolás.

————. *Teatro y sociedad en el Madrid del siglo XVIII*. Madrid: Castalia, 1976. Excellent study of the ideology of eighteenth-century drama.

ARCE, JOAQUÍN. "Rococó, neoclasicismo y prerromanticismo en la poesía española del siglo XVIII." *Cuadernos de la Cátedra Feijoo*, 18 (1966), 447–77. Notes the three trends.

CASO GONZÁLEZ, JOSÉ. "Rococó, preromanticismo y neoclasicismo en el teatro español del siglo XVIII." *Cuadernos de la Cátedra Feijoo*, 22 (1970), 7–29. Contains interesting study of *La petimetra* as a Rococo drama.

CIAN, VITTORIO. *Italia e Spagna nel secolo XVIII: Giovambattista Conti e alcune relazioni letterarie fra l'Italia e la Spagna nella seconda metà del settecento*. Torino: S. Lattes, 1896. Conti was a friend of Moratín.

CIPLIJAUSKAITE, BIRUTÉ. "Lo nacional en el siglo XVIII español." *Archivum*, 22 (1972), 99–121. Underlines importance of nationalism.

COOK, JOHN A. *Neo-Classic Drama in Spain*. Dallas: Southern Methodist University Press, 1959. Fundamental.

COSSÍO, JOSÉ MARÍA DE. *Los toros*. 3 volumes. Madrid: Espasa Calpe, 1943. Masterful study of the bullfight.

————. *Los toros en la poesía española*. 2 volumes. Madrid: Compañía Ibero-Americana, 1931. Discusses Moratín's bullfight works.

COTARELO Y MORI, EMILIO. *Don Ramón de la Cruz y sus obras*. Madrid: J. Perales y Martínez, 1899. Contains useful information about the theatrical controversies of the day.

————. *Iriarte y su época*. Madrid: Sucesores de Rivadeneyra, 1897. Fundamental.

————. *María Ladvenant y Quirante, primera dama de los teatros de la corte*. Madrid: Sucesores de Rivadeneyra, 1896. Dorisa's sister.

COX, R. MERRITT. *Tomás de Iriarte*. New York: Twayne, 1972. Good study of one of Moratín's friends.

DÉROZIER, ALBERT. *Manuel Josef Quintana et la naissance du libéralisme en Espagne*. 2 volumes. Paris: Les Belles Lettres, 1968. Contains interesting discussion of Pelayo theme.

DÍAZ PLAJA, FERNANDO. *La vida española en el siglo XVIII*. Barcelona: Alberto Martín, 1946. How they lived.

DÍAZ PLAJA, GUILLERMO, ed. *Historia general de las literaturas hispánicas*. 7 volumes. Barcelona: Vergara, 1967–69. Very good articles by F. Lázaro Carreter and Agustín del Saz.

DÍEZ BORQUE, J. M., ed. *Historia de la literatura española*. 3 volumes. Madrid: Guadiana, 1975. Valuable contributions by Elena Catena, José Caso González, Joaquín Arce, and René Andioc.

DOWLING, JOHN C. *Leandro Fernández de Moratín*. New York: Twayne, 1971. Good study of Leandro.

————. "Moratín suplicante: La primera carta conocida de don

Leandro." *Revista de Archivos, Bibliotecas y Museos,* 68 (1960), 499-503. Useful document; reveals family details.

————. "A Poet Rewrites History: Nicolás Fernández de Moratín and the Burning of Cortés's Ships." *South Atlantic Bulletin,* 16 (1976), 66-73. Moratín was first to propagate idea that Cortés burned his ships.

————. "The Taurine Works of Nicolás Fernández de Moratín." *South Central Bulletin,* 22 (1962), 31-34. General review of Moratín's interest in the bullfight.

————. "El texto primitivo de *Las naves de Cortés destruidas.*" *Boletín de la Real Academia Española,* 57 (1977), 431-83. First time Moratín's manuscript is published; excellent study.

————. "Tres versiones de *Las naves de Cortés destruidas* de Nicolás Fernández de Moratín." To appear in *Homenaje a Agapito Rey.* Repeats much of what was said in "Texto primitivo," with some new insights.

ENTRAMBASAGUAS, JOAQUÍN DE. *El Madrid de Moratín.* Madrid: Instituto de Estudios Madrileños, 1960. Where Leandro lived.

FERNÁNDEZ GUERRA, AURELIANO. *Lección poética sobre las celebérrimas quintillas de D. Nicolás Fernández de Moratín.* Madrid: Manuel Hernández, 1883. Reprint from *Revista Hispano-Americana,* 18 (1882). Publishes original version; compares it to the one published by Leandro.

GIES, DAVID THATCHER. "'El cantor de las doncellas' y las rameras madrileñas: Nicolás Fernández de Moratín en *El arte de las putas.*" *Actas del 6º Congreso Internacional de Hispanistas* (Toronto, in press). Autobiographical elements in the poem.

GLENDINNING, NIGEL. *A Literary History of Spain: The Eighteenth Century.* New York: Barnes and Noble, 1972. Excellent general study.

————. *Vida y obra de Cadalso.* Madrid: Gredos, 1962. Study of Moratín's good friend.

GÓMEZ DE LA SERNA, GASPAR. "Goya y los toros." *La Estafeta Literaria,* 484 (1972), 4-9; 485 (1972), 12-16. Discusses "Carta Histórica."

GONZÁLEZ PALENCIA, ANGEL. *Entre dos siglos.* Madrid: CSIC, 1943. Studies of Vaca de Guzmán and the Fonda de San Sebastián.

HELMAN, EDITH. "The Elder Moratín and Goya." *Hispanic Review,* 23 (1955), 219-30. First study of *El arte de las putas.*

JULIÁ MARTÍNEZ, E. "Documentos sobre María y Francisca Ladvenant." *Boletín de la Real Academia Española,* 1 (1914), 468-69. Dorisa's death certificate.

LAFUENTE FERRARI, ENRIQUE. "Ilustración y elaboración en la 'Tauromaquia' de Goya." *Archivo español de arte,* 75 (1946), 177-216. Superb study of Goya's sources, which included the "Carta histórica."

LÁZARO CARRETER, FERNANDO. "La transmisión textual de 'Fiesta de toros en Madrid.'" *Clavileño,* 4 (1953), 33-38. Shows how Leandro "corrected" the poem.

MANCINI, GIANCARLO G. "Perfil de Leandro Fernández de Moratín." *Dos estudios de literatura española.* Barcelona: Planeta, 1970. Good amount of information about Nicolás.

MCCLELLAND, IVY L. *The Origins of the Romantic Movement in Spain.* Liverpool: Institute of Hispanic Studies, 1937. Superceded by *Spanish Drama of Pathos* but still contains very useful material.

―――. *Spanish Drama of Pathos, 1750-1808.* Two volumes. Toronto: University Press, 1970. Excellent study of eighteenth-century drama.

MENÉNDEZ PELAYO, MARCELINO. *Historia de las ideas estéticas en España.* 5 volumes. Santander: Aldus, 1940. Opinionated but worthy study, particularly of the controversy over the *autos.*

―――. *Horacio en España.* 2 volumes. Madrid: A. Pérez Dubrull, 1885. Moratín's translations of Horace.

MESONERO ROMANOS, RAMÓN DE. *Trabajos no coleccionados.* Two volumes. Madrid, 1903-1905. Presents several interesting biographical details.

MININNI, CARMINE G. *Pietro Napoli Signorelli: Vita, opere, tempi, amici.* Castello: S. Lapi, 1914. A friend of Moratín recalled.

MOORE, JOHN. *Ramón de la Cruz.* New York: Twayne, 1972. Competent synthesis of Cruz's activities.

MORATÍN, LEANDRO FERNÁNDEZ DE. "Fragmento de la vida de Moratín." *Obras póstumas.* Three volumes. Madrid: Rivadeneyra, 1867. Short but revealing insights into his early life.

NAPOLI SIGNORELLI, PIETRO. *Storia critica de'teatri antichi e moderni.* Naples, 1777. Work influenced by Moratín; presents short opinions of Moratín's plays. Reprinted in 1787-90, 1813.

PAGEAUX, DANIEL-HENRI. "Le thème de la résistance asturienne dans la tragédie néo-classique espagnole." *Mélanges à la mémoire de Jean Sarrailh,* 2. Paris, 1966, 235-42. The Pelayo theme in Spain.

PEERS, EDGAR ALLISON. *A History of the Romantic Movement in Spain.* Two volumes. Cambridge: Cambridge University Press, 1940. Stretches the case with Moratín, but still contains a wealth of information.

PELLISSIER, ROBERT E. *The Neo-Classic Movement in Spain During the Eighteenth Century.* California: Stanford University Press, 1918. Contains a short synopsis of Moratín's career.

PÉREZ DE GUZMÁN, J. "El padre de Moratín." *La España Moderna,* June 1900, 16-33. Interesting view of Nicolás.

SEBOLD, RUSSELL P. *Coronel Don José Cadalso.* New York: Twayne, 1971. Translated: Gredos, 1974. Excellent details.

―――. "Contra los mitos antineoclásicos españoles." *Papeles de Son*

Armadans, 35 (1964), 85–114. Fundamental defense of eighteenth-century literature.

———. "Introducción" to Ignacio López de Ayala, *Numancia destruida.* Salamanca: Anaya, 1971. Solid information about one of Moratín's friends.

SEMPERE Y GUARINOS, J. *Ensayo de una biblioteca de los mejores escritores del reinado de Carlos III.* Six volumes. Madrid: Imprenta Real, 1785–89. Reprinted by Gredos, 1969. Contains a contemporary bibliographical view of Nicolás.

SERRANO Y SAZ, M. "El Consejo de Castilla y la censura de libros en el siglo XVIII." *Revista de Archivos, Bibliotecas y Museos,* 15 (1906), 28–46, 243–59, 387–402; 16 (1907), 180–16, 206–18. Some information on Nicolás as a literary censor.

SILVELA, MANUEL. "Vida de don Leandro Fernández de Moratín." *Obras póstumas de D. Leandro Fernández de Moratín.* Two volumes. Madrid: Rivadeneyra, 1867. Silvela writes of Leandro's memories of his father.

SIMÓN DÍAZ, JOSÉ. *Historia del Colegio Imperial de Madrid.* Two volumes. Madrid: CSIC, 1952–59. Excellent study of the Imperial College.

———. "Nicolás Fernández de Moratín, opositor a cátedras." *Revista de Filología Española,* 28 (1944) 154–76. Nicolás's attempts to secure a position at the Imperial College.

SOUBEYROUX, JACQUES. "Des bienfaits de la corrida en Espagne au XVIIIe siècle." *Bulletin Hispanique,* 76 (1974), 183–91. The polemic over the bullfight.

Additional bibliographical information can be found in the Notes and References section.

Index